THE ECHO FACTOR

LIVING A LIFE THAT RESONATES FREEDOM

...

By Kinda Wilson

To Clint AKA Devo — Hope you enjoy! my crazy stories! Honored to have you read. May you Follow your truth & resonate freedom Kida arts

Scripture taken from The Message. Copyright © 1993, 1994, 1995, 1996, 2000, 2001, 2002. Used by permission of NavPress Publishing Group.

Box Cover Design: Sarah Sung
Design Work and Illustrations: Jessica Allée
Editor: Shayla Eaton of Curiouser Editing

1 2 3 4 5 6 7 8 9 10 11 12 13 14 15

ISBN: 978-0-9968464-0-0
Copyright by Kinda Wilson, 2015
Published by

Spotted Elephant Publishing
www.spottedelephantpublishing.com

....

*To all of the people who have echoed into my life.
My amazing friends and my incredible family—Mom, Dad,
Garret, Grandma—you have impacted every area of my life,
and I only hope to be able to pass along what you have given
me.*

. . . .

THE ECHO FACTOR

PART I

BEING A VOICE

....

ECHO [EK-OH]

...

1. (noun)
A person who slavishly repeats
the words or opinions of another.

...

2. (verb)
Repeat (someone's words or opinions),
typically to express agreement.

...

"These criticisms are echoed
in a number of other studies."

PERSONAL NOTES

SUBJECT _Learning Lessons in the Pieces_
YEAR _Not Too Long Ago_

I suppose, to tell you my stories, I should start somewhere in the middle and then move to the beginning before you can understand the end.

Life is a lot less linear than I thought it would be.

And lessons aren't learned in step-by-step fashion as I was so confident would happen. The pieces are picked up one by one, here and there, and strung together in crookedly formed lines of recognition and reasoning. They're stacked up in neglected corners until the pieces are called upon to fill an aptly shaped void in one of life's puzzles. That's how we learn lessons.

That's what life has been like for me, anyway. Less about a steady progression of things. More about puzzle-solving. More about pieces I've picked up along the way slowly connecting together and sinking in to form subtle epiphanies. I've always wanted answers, and life has always given me puzzles.

And that's where I found myself on a Tuesday afternoon—puzzle-solving, if you will, in the most unlikely of places.

....

I can't tell you one single story to perfectly explain how my life had led up to that moment, that decision, that puzzle.

That lesson.

But I can start somewhere near the middle.

And I can give you the pieces.

PERSONAL NOTES

SUBJECT *Lilac and Magenta*

YEAR *Not Too Long Ago*

I was about to meet a grandmother who would change my world. I was about to rethink my clothing collection. And it came completely out of the clear blue Italian sky.

There I stood looking at my dream: Manarola, Cinque de Terra, Italy. The brightly colored houses stacked in close to each other, hugging the sides of the cliffs overlooking the sea. They spread across the hill like a rustic Italian rainbow.

For years I had heard about hiking the trails of Cinque de Terre, "Five Lands" as it was called. Five little towns were strung along the Italian coastline with a tiny footpath stretching between them. Rumor had it that a hundred years ago, lovers from neighboring towns would meet each other halfway on the footpath.

I considered hiking between the towns after dark on the footpath of love, just in case someone was waiting there for me. With my luck, it would be a mugger.

I looked out over Manarola, Italy, and decided I had never seen anything so beautiful.

....

An hour later, actually climbing the hill to get to my hostel wasn't quite as beautiful. I was weak and pale and spindly. Plus, I had overpacked for the entire trip. I looked like a giant Popsicle about to tip over.

I stumbled up the hill with the gigantic pack on my back. A little old lady lightly trotted up past me—her calves looked like those of a linebacker. Amazing. I was pretty sure she ate seven hundred grams of glorious Italian carbs a day and was going to live forever. My friend Annie was traveling with me and was extremely amused by my lack of leg power. *This seems to be a theme in my travels...*

Annie and I bought tickets to hike the famous trails of Cinque de Terre and took off. We trekked along the winding path connecting the villages. Annie kept slowing down to wait for me. Much older people zipped around me like it was nothing. One elderly man taunted me on the way. "You're young. You should be running circles around us!"

I huffed out what was meant to be a clever retort and then bent over to catch my breath again. Really? Was I this out of shape? Pathetic. I sweated some more but kept going.

And then it happened—the moment that is forever stuck in my mind in hues of lilac and magenta.

About halfway to the town of Vernazza, we came upon a group of five elderly ladies who were also hiking. Great-grandmothers to be sure, and French, I think. They had become too hot on the trail and had stripped off their shirts down to their undergarments—bright pink magenta with lilac flowers for one of the ladies.

....

Annie and I looked at each other and bit back a laugh. We were both thinking the same thing. *This lady is my grandma's age, and she's hiking a trail in a flowered bra.* The lady was just walking, chattering, and carrying on without a care in the world.

I've gotta admit, something in me just said, *Yessss. You go, girls!* They wanted to climb the hill and were going to do it however they needed to. People's opinions be hanged. I wanted to be that gutsy. I wanted to find that rebel in me and just charge ahead with living life and reveling in the craziness of it all. I'm not saying I wanted the flowered-bra hike, but I wanted their attitude.

I wanted to care a little bit less about what everyone thought of my dream. I wanted to power on regardless of the voices around me. I wanted to feel that comfortable in my own skin and walk with that kind of confidence.

I look back now and wish I would have talked to them. I wish I would have stopped and asked for their names. I wish I would have hung out with them for an afternoon to see if some of their gumption would have rubbed off on me.

Instead, Annie and I did the only thing that came to mind that our bravery allowed—we decided to sneak a snapshot to remember them by. Annie looked at me again, and I knew what she was getting ready to do. "Hey, Kinda, let me take a picture of you on the path," she yelled at me from farther down the trail. I moved off to the side, making sure she could get the ladies in the picture. She took the picture, and we both hiked off, grinning. We had a memento of the day.

....

I knew one thing for sure after that hike. I didn't want to wait until I was Lilac and Magenta's age to have that much freedom. I wanted to live that freely *now*.

To figure out how, I would need to do a little digging through a few centuries of research. No big deal. And it would start with a television show in the 1960s.

To Lilac and Magenta on the trail:

You don't know me, but I want to be more like you. I want to be confident in my voice. I want the blissful oblivion to all of the extra junk that I worry about. The living life for the adventure and not for the other passersby on the trail. I promise you I will do something a little extra-crazy and a little extra-me this week and enjoy. every. single. second.

....

RESEARCH NOTES

SUBJECT _Face the Rear_

YEAR _1962_

Candid Camera didn't know it yet, but it was getting ready to record one of its most famous television shows of all time, "Face the Rear." The year was 1962, and the show's producers had rigged an elevator with hidden cameras for its newest experiment.[1]

It was a normal workday morning, and people were dressed in slacks and trench coats. A few people even sported fashionable hats. This detail would be important later on in the show. As the show began filming, the elevator stood with doors closed, awaiting the business rush of the day. The first victim—er, subject—punched the elevator button, waited until the doors opened, and then strode confidently into the elevator.

· 62 ·

Then at least three people, all cohorts of the *Candid Camera* show, stepped into the elevator . . . and faced the rear.

Now everyone knows what is supposed to happen when you walk into an elevator. If you're the first person in, you hit the button of the correct floor and walk to the back of the elevator . . . and turn around and face the door. You look at the door, your phone, or the lights flashing above you. No one ever stands near anyone else unless he or she absolutely has to. You most certainly don't turn around and look at other people.

And, unless there's a giant mirror on the wall, no one ever, ever faces the rear of the elevator.

But back to the show. The first subject was now in an elevator, standing at the back, and facing the "correct" way—toward the door. The other three people were in the elevator with him, facing him, and facing the rear.

The subject shuffled a bit. He fidgeted and wiped his mouth with his hand. He reached up and nervously touched his brow. He moved his hand across his mouth again and his eyes darted quickly around the elevator. You could almost see him frantically trying to make sense of the situation.

The man pulled up his sleeve and looked at his watch and slowly rotated his body . . . until he was facing the rear. This entire scenario took less than a minute. At the end, the man still had no idea why he was facing the opposite direction from the door, but he was facing that way all the same.

. . . .

Candid Camera pulled this stunt over and over, each time getting similar results. At one point, they had an elevator full of men pulling their hats off and on in unison—and the unknowing subject following right with them. Other subjects were steered in entire circles while in the elevator.

In fact, if you watched that episode, you would question if these were people at all. They turned and spun and de-hatted and re-hatted quite elegantly, almost as if you were watching an orchestrated show of dolphins at an aquarium.

You would probably also question if these results were fabricated. Surely people would need a reason to turn in circles in an elevator, wouldn't they? But the show's producers knew something about human behavior that most people didn't know.

They had heard of Solomon Asch.

Candid Camera Video Clip:
www.kindawilson.com/candid-camera

RESEARCH NOTES

SUBJECT _Solomon Asch & His Grand Experiment_

YEAR _1950_

Solomon Asch. I was holding his secrets.

I felt the weight of the stacks of paper in my hands, full up, paper-clipped, and shrouding mysteries. I giggled a bit at what I had found and then giggled again at how badly I was geeking out.

At least I had an awareness of it.

Yes, my hands held mysteries, but not the normal ones that you would see on _CSI_, mind you. The kind of mysteries you wonder about when you look at someone's life decisions and shake your head and try to figure out what the heck they're thinking. The kind of mysteries where you ponder what pushes someone's mind to the very brink of disaster or pulls it out of contentment and throws it into restless wander.

Those were the mysteries that had always fascinated me: the thoughts and motivations that happened in people's heads.

In middle school, I put together science projects to see if I could influence people with subliminal messages. I ended up embedding messages into

. . . .

everything from computer programs to spaghetti advertisements. In one experiment, I had subjects take a pretend computer survey while a number flashed in the background, just below conscious level. I wanted to see if it would influence their random number choices. In another experiment, I embedded the word *buy* onto the pictures on spaghetti boxes to see if it affected people's purchasing decisions.

My methods were embarrassingly unscientific—people have favorite numbers, after all—but the curiosity was there. And I'll never look at a box of spaghetti now without suspiciously searching for messages.

Now here I was as an adult, holding stacks of unpublished personal letters, handwritten notes, and documents by another curious person—a psychologist by the name of Solomon Asch. I was looking into the mind of someone who was looking into the mind of someone. I thought about that a bit and things went a little *Inception* on me.

If there were anyone whose work I wanted to study, it would be this guy's.

Solomon Asch had performed an experiment in the 1950s that had taken the psychology world by storm. So much so that the *Candid Camera* producers would remember it a full decade later and base an entire episode on it. So much so that I would read about it in my Psychology 101 textbooks in college and then track down the Solomon Asch Foundation years later and order stacks of his personal notes and unpublished memos to read through.

It was considered ground-breaking, this experiment, but it appeared

....

quite innocent on the surface.

Solomon Asch gave college students a vision test. (Or that's what he said he was doing. But he was trickier than that.) He began his experiment by asking people to match line lengths.[2]

It was such a simple test that the subjects chose the right answer over 99% of the time. And over 95% of the people got all of the answers correct.[3] But things were about to get interesting.

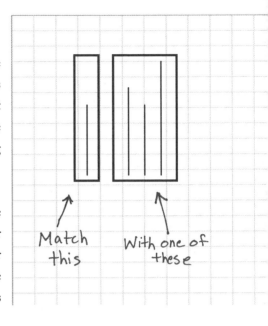

Match this

With one of these

Solomon Asch added one thing to his experiment—one thing—and suddenly people were missing those easy questions like crazy. The percentage of people getting perfect scores dropped from 95% to 25%.[4]

What did Asch do to cause this? He added peers.

It turns out this vision experiment wasn't about vision at all. It was about independence and conformity. Trick-y.

To create an element of pressure to conform, Asch added seven to nine other people in the room while the subject took the vision test. They all took the test at the same time, and they all had to answer (one at a time) *out loud*. Plus, the subject was placed in the next-to-the-last chair in the row. This means the subject would hear almost everyone else's answer before he responded.[5]

....

No pressure, right? Suddenly, things weren't so simple anymore.

I read through Solomon Asch's research notes as he documented the confused thoughts of the subjects in their exit interviews.

You could almost hear the exact moment when each subject realized something was wrong. It was a prequel to the elevator stunt, only the nervousness was magnified and spotlighted and slowed down into painful slow motion.

Each time that the peers answered incorrectly, the subject knew his turn was coming. He knew that in a matter of seconds he would be put on the spot. You can read the internal terror in the words and the moments of resignation when each one decided to answer with the crowd.

....

Over and over, the subjects answered the same as those around them . . . all the while looking at cards where the answer was obvious and right in front of their faces.

As I read through the notes from the experiment, as one subject after another went with the majority and answered incorrectly, another story flashed through my mind—one from hundreds of years before.

It was the story of a beautiful young woman who lived in the mountains.

---

con.form.i.ty [kuhn-fawr-mi-tee]
noun, plural con.form.i.ties.

action in accord with prevailing social standards, attitudes, practices, etc.

correspondence in form, nature, or character; agreement, congruity, or accordance.

compliance or acquiescence; obedience.

....

RESPONSES[6]
(recorded by Solomon Asch research team, 1950)

"I was beginning to think that '140 million Frenchmen can't be wrong,' which is hypocritical, of course."

"After all, the majority rules, so I guess I was wrong."

"First I thought something was the matter with me or most of them . . . I was sure they were wrong, but not sure I was right."

"Everybody here's crazy but me! . . . seeing they had the power of numbers, I thought they must be right somehow, but it wasn't what I saw and I think I was right."

"I felt like a silly fool." ⟵

"I felt conspicuous, going out on a limb, and subjecting myself to criticism that my perceptions, faculties were not as acute as they might be."

"I felt I wanted to go along with the crowd. I didn't want to seem different."

"One subject described how he wanted to be independent, but 'the closer it got to me the great the compulsion (not to differ).'"

RESEARCH NOTES

SUBJECT _Greek Mythology_

YEAR _Ancient Times_

Hundreds of years before Solomon Asch was even a twinkle in his parents' eyes, a Greek tale was being born about a beautiful young woman who lived in the mountains.[7]

This lady was charming and loved to talk with everyone. She was full of wit and had to have the last word in edgewise. You could say she loved the sound of her own voice. During the day, she chatted with her friends about flowers and life and skinny jeans. (I may have taken a bit of liberty with this story.)

The beautiful young woman eventually met and became friends with the goddess Hera, wife of the famous Zeus.

One day she decided to trick Hera. She distracted Hera by telling her stories while Hera's husband ran off and cheated on her. Granted, it was a pretty low stunt that she pulled, and Hera was so furious that she placed a curse upon the young woman.

The curse was this: the girl could never again speak what she wanted to say. She could never again tell her own thoughts. All she could do was

....

repeat parts of phrases that were spoken to her. That's it.

As you might guess, things got awkward pretty quickly. The girl couldn't say if she enjoyed a meal or if she hated the weather unless others around her spoke the same things first. I can't even imagine what life must have been like or what embarrassing situations she encountered.

Soon she fell in love with a handsome guy by the name of Narcissus; he was strong and amazing and all things manly. The young girl longed to tell Narcissus that she spent her days daydreaming about him and doodling their names together in spiral notebooks, but because of the curse placed upon her, she couldn't speak her own words.

Then one day, straight out of a creepy vampire love/stalker scene, she followed Narcissus into the woods. That's when awkward boosted to epic levels.

Narcissus: Who's there?
Young woman: Who's there?
Narcissus: Why do you run from me?
Young woman: . . . run from me?

Then, yada yada, and the girl was chasing the poor guy through the woods and throwing herself at him like a teenage girl at a boy band concert. She wasn't much for subtlety in relationships.

The story goes on and eventually ends with the girl dying a broken-hearted tragic death. A little melodramatic, if you ask me. But thus the legend was born. A girl who was only given permission to speak if someone else spoke the same thing first. A girl never again to be herself unless someone else gave her permission.

A girl who couldn't be the unique person she was created to be—a girl who was only allowed to speak if the world around her agreed.

And her name?

Her name was Echo.

"Scorned, she wanders in the woods and hides her face in shame among the leaves, and from that time she lives on in lonely caves, increased by the sadness of rejection. Her sleepless thoughts waste her sad form, and her body's strength vanishes into the air. Only her bones and the sound of her voice are left. Her voice remains, her bones, they say, were changed to shapes of stone. She hides in the woods, no longer to be seen on the hills, but to be heard by everyone. It is the sound that lives in her."

. . . .

```
┌────────────────────────────────────────────────────────┐
│                                                          │
│           P E R S O N A L   N O T E S                    │
│                                                          │
│   SUBJECT  Me Being Echo                                 │
│   YEAR     Present Day                                    │
│                                                          │
└────────────────────────────────────────────────────────┘
```

I remember first reading that story and shaking my head. It didn't sound like much of a myth at all, much less Greek. Especially if I pictured it with the skinny jeans added in.

I identified with Echo much more than I wanted to admit. I had often felt nervous or scared to voice my opinions when I thought others would disagree—or even when I felt they might support me. I was nervous about being myself in general. I didn't want to feel silly or look stupid, so I had tried to reflect everyone around me.

Back in high school and college when an instructor asked a question, I would be terrified to raise my hand. That was odd, because I usually had at least one or two thoughts to add to the class discussion. But there was something about raising my hand that said, "Here! Look here! I have something important to say and everyone should focus on me and judge my words!" I disagreed many times in my head, but I let it go.

Once in college, I was called in to speak to one of the officials at the university about a request I had made. I walked into his office and sat down. I'll leave most of the details out, but I will say what happened at

....

the end: he said he thought I felt overly sure that my request would be approved. And for that reason, they were turning me down. He implied that, based on his assessment of my demeanor, I was a bit entitled.

Every fiber of my being screamed in appalled disagreement and justified rage, but I felt stunned and paralyzed. I must have nodded in reply. He waved his finger in front of my face.

"See there?" he said. "That's it. You don't think the answer is any different. You see what I mean, then? You agree as well! You don't even seem to care to fight. You're even apathetic about this."

And I nodded. And I said yes. And I went on.

I still have knots form in my stomach as I recall it.

If I could go back in time, I would level a million things back at him. I would tell him that I pick my battles and that I adamantly disagreed. I would tell him he was completely wrong in his assessment of me. I would tell him he lost a great asset in passing me over.

Confident or shaking, I would have stood up to him.

But I didn't.

I walked away.

I let him decide my words for the day.

I had merely echoed.

....

But it went beyond just a singular meeting with an official in college. I had been terrified of being myself for a long time. It had been easier just to walk and talk like those surrounding me. They spoke, and I echoed. They voiced an opinion, and I agreed. They made crazy nineties hair bangs, and I made mine higher. (Note as to why I don't share pictures from the nineties.)

It would have been different had I actually wanted to be all of those people—if I had agreed with what they were telling me.

But I hadn't. I hadn't wanted to be those things at all. I had believed entirely different things in my head. I had wanted to be an entirely *different person* in my head.

I had been trying so hard to get their approval that I had become a character of Greek mythological proportions. I had become an Echo.

....

```
┌─────────────────────────────────────────────┐
│                                               │
│         RESEARCH NOTES                        │
│                                               │
│   SUBJECT  Finding a Voice                    │
│   YEAR     1950 - Now                         │
│                                               │
└─────────────────────────────────────────────┘
```

As I read through the notes of the Asch Independence and Conformity Experiment again, I couldn't help but think that the subjects had become Greek Echoes as well. No, they didn't have curses placed on them, per se. No Greek goddess was hovering in the background and singing "I Put a Spell on You." Although that would have made the experiment even more interesting.

But still—curse or no curse—it was almost as if they had lost the ability to say what they wanted. They had lost their voices. They had become Echoes.

And when the psychology community got wind of the Asch Experiment in the 1950s, many agreed with that assessment. The science journals predominantly said the same thing: people conform when it's difficult. They succumb to peer pressure. The world speaks, and the people echo. In fact, the psychology community nicknamed Asch's work the "Conformity Experiments."[8]

However, that was only half of the tale. If you look deeper, conformity wasn't the entirety of what Solomon Asch set out to find; there was a

....

behind-the-scenes story. He didn't want to just know what made people echo—he wanted to know what made people have a *voice*.

But the psychology community—intentionally or unintentionally—was leaving out this crucial element of his research. Solomon Asch wasn't happy about it at all, as he talked about in the rough draft of his work "Freedom, Independence and Conformity."[9]

"When I came to this problem I was struck by what seemed a singular omission. So impressed were social psychologists with the powers of conformity that there was virtually no reference to those forces that make for independence of thought and action . . . This omission determined the direction of my inquiries: I wanted to find a place for independence of group demands in the operation of social forces.

"Over the years I began increasingly to notice that psychologists were referring to my 'conformity' studies. At first I tried to correct them; being polite they accepted this gracefully although sometimes with a slight sense of shock and embarrassment. Later I had to conclude that my correction was simply useless, that I was face to face with a social current. The people who banded together as social psychologists were interested, ~~qua social psychologists,~~ in conformity, not independence. I stopped correcting them. ~~and gradually I noticed that I was decreasing my attendance at psychological meetings"~~

Wait wait— Does this mean Solomon Asch himself conformed here?

Interestingly enough, the psychology community had conformed about . . . conformity.

. . . .

Looking at the cultural landscape surrounding Solomon Asch during his early years, you can see why both conformance and independence were such important topics for the scientific community and for society at large.

His buddies called him "Shlaym"- I think we could have been pals.

Solomon Asch was born in Warsaw, Poland, in 1907 and had grown up the son of a Jewish couple in the city of Lowicz.[10] In the 1920s, Asch and his family emigrated to the United States. Asch described his upbringing as being a "small religious environment where the relation of people to the forces around them was very real. In that setting, man is very important, not just to himself, he's important in the scheme of things, and this feeds an interest in human nature."[11]

Take the picture larger past the small familial environment of Asch, and you can see the stark reality of just how important man was in the scheme of things during that time period. The world was in an upheaval. Nations watched as Hitler and his reign of evil and terror took over an entire region. Droves of people fell prey to Hitler's propaganda tactics. In fact, some of Asch's first research was aimed at investigating influence related to propaganda.[12]

Gruber, a friend and colleague of Asch, left for the army in 1943 in the midst of war and heard about the independence and conformity work from afar.

> Asch was beginning his group pressure work just as I left for the army in January or February of 1943. The word reached me from friends: "people stick to their guns!" It was electrifying. Then he moved from Brooklyn College and started finding that the number of "yielders"—even in this perceptually highly structured situation—was disappointingly large.

....

We have all had to learn to swallow that result, along with the lessons of the Nazi successes, and Zimbardo's and Milgrim's experiments, telling us that evil conformity is international.[13]

"Evil conformity"—this was the culture that surrounded Asch. But he didn't just want to know if people were susceptible to surrounding pressure—they were; everyone knew that. It was obvious. The widespread swastika armbands across Germany were proof enough of that.

Asch also wanted to know what made someone stand strong in the midst of conforming forces.

So Asch went back to his experiment results. And in true Nancy Drew fashion, he dug deeper. In the midst of the initial shock of the realization that so many people had chosen wrong, Asch found something else: there had been a group who had stuck to their guns and chosen the right answers. And even among the people who had answered wrong, they had *still* answered right much of the time, even against their peers.[14]

That was a group that Asch wanted to learn more about. What made them stand up for what they believed? Were they not uncomfortable? Did they not question themselves? Here was a small-scale example of independence under pressure, and people had stood their ground.

What made them different? Was it education, income, personality type, burned-in genetic DNA structure? What was the magic DNA or environment formula for bravery?

And there it was—the strange and uncomfortable answer . . .

. . . .

There was no brave personality type or DNA structure. None at all.

And even beyond that, many people who had remained independent—who had stood strong—didn't have some amazing internal oblivion to the pressure around them. In fact, many of them had the exact same doubts as those who yielded to the peer pressure.

RESPONSES: PEOPLE WHO WERE INDEPENDENT YET HAD DOUBTS[15]

"I began to question whether my own perception was as acute as it seemed to be."

"You have doubts when you finish a thing like that."

It's like "gaslighting"!

Yes, they had doubts. The difference, Asch realized, was what they did with the doubts, as he explained in his research publication. "Most subjects felt concern over the disagreement. Concern bore no relation to performance. What differentiated between the subjects was not the presence of concern but the ways in which they dealt with it."

How had they dealt with it? I looked closely at the responses to try to formulate an answer, and I noticed similarities in some of them: they recognized the doubts they had. They decided ahead of time to go with

. . . .

their intuition. And they called upon everything within them to stick it out—even though it was uncomfortable.

RESPONSES: PEOPLE WHO STOOD THEIR GROUND[16]

"I was confident at first, then became doubtful. Then I made my decision before I heard anyone else and stuck to it to remove the danger of following the leader."

"I demanded of myself to have the courage of my convictions. I pulled myself together and said: 'Regardless of what the others say I'll report what my eyes tell me.' I had to build up a certain amount of defiance to give a different answer."

To add another layer, Asch explained in his "Freedom, Independence and Conformity"[17] paper that there seemed to be a fundamental difference in what forces lay behind someone's conformity or independence.

Asch came to the conclusion that conformity related to an outside force, being afraid of something external. While independence was based on an internal force, a quest for truth. Plus, he thought there was another concept he felt social psychology had no real framework for: freedom.

It seemed to me then that conformity was causal, and perhaps freedom was its own thing—the beautiful notion of one's actions being untied from the causes and voices.

....

It was a cartoon lightbulb-over-the-head moment for me. The guys in the experiment had doubts, but they had pulled themselves together. They had relied on internal truth rather than external cues. I pictured my grandma holding up her hand in the shape of a fist and giving me a pep talk. "Come on, girl, you can do it. Pull yourself together, girl!"

And I realized that's what you do. You look at the voices around you. You look at what you know is true. Then you look in the mirror and say, "This is going to be uncomfortable, but come on now. Pull yourself together! You can do it. Be yourself. Be a voice."

Asch's study was called "A Minority of One Against a Unanimous Majority." Gandhi said, "If you are a minority of one, the truth is still the truth." WOW

TRANSLATIONS[18]

Ways to say "pull yourself together" in other cultures

"брать/взять себя в руки", Russian Phrase-Literal translation: To take oneself in one's hands

"Sich zusammenreißen", German Phrase-Literal translation: To tear oneself together

"wziąć się w garść'", Polish Phrase-Translation: We take ourselves into our fist

---

PERSONAL NOTES

SUBJECT My Paradigm Shift

YEAR Present Day

Solomon Asch's Independence and Conformity Study really messed with the paradigm of bravery in my head. For so long I had looked at people and thought, *If only I were a brave person like they are, then I could do what I wanted.* I had pondered, *I wish I were more like them. I wish I were brave like her. Then . . . THEN I could have the guts to say what I think. THEN I could be the person I want to be.*

But this study took away my excuses. I looked over the results of it again. It was true.

There was no brave girl immune to all doubt and questioning. There was just the me I could be if I were willing to be <u>uncomfortable</u>.

And it also meant that if there were no DNA for perfect bravery, then we could all be that brave person.

It meant we *all* had the ability to be brave.

We could all be a voice. We could all have that freedom to act from internal truth.

. . . .

It seemed then that I needed to learn to pull myself together and say some of the things I had been scared to say. And be the me that I had been scared to be. Because I so wanted to be that version of me who was brave.

I had the opportunity to test it out a few weeks later while looking at some broken flower vases.

. . . .

PERSONAL NOTES

SUBJECT Yard Sale

YEAR Present Day

I stood there shaking at the edge of the tag sale, my adrenaline completely maxed out and overwhelming my senses. Usually, I had adrenaline rushes when I found amazing deals, like those designer boots I had picked up for a dollar. A dollar.

Unfortunately, that wasn't the case this time. I continued to stand, looking down, peering sightlessly at all of the rows and rows of knickknacks around me, pretending as if I intensely cared about the half-broken vase that should have been long thrown away.

And the words washed over me, filled the air around me, sung in muted whispers and voices too obvious behind cupped hands. I had almost forgotten that blatant racism existed in the world. I mean, I knew it was there, theoretically, but I wasn't surrounded by it. I didn't hear it. My friends were every shape and color, and a racist mindset was as ridiculous to me as it was foreign. Perhaps I was sheltered.

But here the words were. The ladies stayed huddled at one end of the room; the object of their comments at the other. And I, I stood in the middle, in every sense of the word.

. . . .

My face reddened as I realized the possibility that the seemingly oblivious people might have heard the barbs hurled in their direction. What should I do? I didn't know any of these people. But I knew something that made this situation even more maddening.

The sale that I was attending—the fundraiser sale—was held by the very type of organization that was meant to defend the people it was begrudging.

And I knew then that I couldn't *not* say anything. I couldn't just walk away. And I was terrified.

You would think that years of genetic chutzpah from a sassy maternal bloodline would have rubbed off on me. And perhaps it had in some fashion, but I realized that if I were going to say anything, it would be through shaking lips and a stammering tongue.

I walked over, slowly, eyes down, face twitching in panic, to the table of ladies. My stature showed every sign of terror and none of confidence. This was not my place to say anything to these strangers. And yet . . . maybe it was. I motioned for the lady in charge and asked if I could speak to her in private.

And so it was, with a concerned look on her face, that she led me to the hall.

"T-t-those comments your group was saying, it's not right. It's just not right. I t-t-think this place is supposed to be one of safety and refuge, and those are the very people you're here to help. I'm very protective of what this place stands for. And i-i-it's not right. W-w-what you're saying."

"You thought that was racist? I can't be racist—my family emigrated from Germany."

And the irony washed over me in waves of disbelief.

I finished the conversation and turned and left. I made it to the car before my leg went into full-blown spasms. It turned out learning to speak my voice was harder than I had thought. But that didn't matter. Slowly, a calming realization began to settle in.

I had spoken.

PERSONAL NOTES

SUBJECT Thoughts on Being a Voice

YEAR Present Day

Sometimes being a voice is jumping in and speaking your mind, as I had that day. Sometimes it's standing up for someone when no one else will. And also, sometimes being a voice is quietly being you, 100 percent you, the entire essence of you, regardless of anything else around you.

It's not getting caught up in every distraction or drama or disagreement that would pull you away from your purpose.

That's also what being a voice is.

And I discovered that from two guys from a long time ago and a not-so-long-ago sale at a clothing store.

RESEARCH NOTES

SUBJECT___Giving a Meh___

YEAR___Ancient Times___

In biblical times (the early ADs, that is), two guys by the name of Paul and Barnabas set off on a grand cross-country adventure, traveling from town to town on Vespas and teaching religious groups of their time. Or they were on foot, one of the two.

They ended up stopping in a town called Antioch in Pisidia.[19]

Antioch is now the city called Antakya in South-Central Turkey. At the time, Antioch was a thriving center for commerce and culture. It was the third largest city in the Roman Empire and had theaters, aqueducts, and grand temples.

Antioch was quite the place to be—people apparently liked things like aqueducts. It wasn't any wonder then, if Paul and Barnabas had wanted to be teachers and cultural influences, that they would have chosen Antioch as a stop on their journey.

So there they were, in the center of all the hubbub of the day. Soon after they arrived in Antioch, they attended a meeting place on the Sabbath, and the president of the meeting asked them to speak.[20]

....

As one telling of the day puts it, the leader turned to them and asked, "Friends, do you have anything you want to say? A word of encouragement, perhaps?"

He had asked the right people, as Paul was rarely short on stuff to say. The guy was a talker, after all. After Paul shared (and shared), the meeting ended and Paul and Barnabas were invited back for the next Sabbath.

But not everyone was pleased with their message. Some of the townspeople were alarmed and started talking about them. A whisper campaign, if you will. People talking, taking sides. I don't know how word spread so quickly without the Internet, but it did. The week continued and the people's unrest grew. By the time the Sabbath rolled around again, the townspeople forced Paul and Barnabas to leave.[21]

Let's just think about that for a second. The townspeople didn't agree with what they were saying. And they threw them out of town.

So Paul and Barnabas stopped sharing their words and started a social media war.

No they didn't. That must have been some other guys.

As one writer put it, they "shrugged their shoulders" and went on their way, "brimming with joy."[22]

Um . . . what?

....

....

I paused when I read that part of the story.

They didn't get distracted. They didn't stop what they were doing to engage in the mindsets of those around them. They just kept going.

I picture a little flannel-board Barnabas saying, "Meh!" and skipping happily along the path. I know—I'm sure he didn't skip in those biblical sandals, but I see that picture all the same. And if you follow that up with an "Ain't nobody got time for dat," crossed with an Old Testament-style Taylor Swift "Shake It Off," you'll see what happens in my head.

What can I say? I was inspired by these guys.

Looking at the context of the story, I was inspired to the point of puzzled. It wasn't that they were happy because there was nothing to be worried about. In fact, in the very next town, Paul was stoned—and I mean people threw actual rocks at him—and left for dead at the edge of town. He lived, but barely.[23]

Those risks might have been there, and I'm sure Paul and Barnabas were aware of them. But they hadn't focused on the voices around them or the distractions. They focused on what they believed. They focused on what they were meant to say and on being who they were meant to be.

They had learned what I had not yet learned: focusing on your passion brings joy. Focusing on the distractions brings worry and frustration.

....

I realized I should take a few pointers from these guys. I had wanted so badly to be liked—for people to approve of who I was—that I had often leaned too heavily on surrounding feedback. I had valued my decisions by the gauge of people's opinions of them.

And I don't mean my mentors—I mean people *who I didn't even want to be like.*

It had been tormenting to my mind. Almost everyone had different opinions on what they thought my life should be like.

I didn't know how Paul and Barnabas had done it, but I wanted their "Meh!" when someone disagreed with my dream. I wanted their "Meh!" when someone didn't approve of me as a person. Their singular focus on a mission.

I wanted to keep my passion and joy when someone disagreed with my voice.

I had the opportunity to test it out a few weeks later, in a way that would give retail therapy a whole new meaning.

....

```
┌─────────────────────────────────────────────┐
│  ┌───────────────────────────────────────┐  │
│  │                                         │  │
│  │         PERSONAL NOTES                  │  │
│  │                                         │  │
│  │  SUBJECT  Shopping Retail Therapy       │  │
│  │  YEAR     Not Too Long Ago              │  │
│  │                                         │  │
│  └───────────────────────────────────────┘  │
└─────────────────────────────────────────────┘
```

"This is all trash. Look at this—this dress is damaged. Why are we even looking here? Hmph, such trash!"

I cocked my head to the side to inconspicuously listen to the middle-aged couple arguing at the end of the aisle. I'm pretty sure they were oblivious to my presence anyway. On and on they continued, arguing about why they were shopping at a bargain outlet. "Don't we need something with more bling? Where is the bling on these dresses? We need bling!"

I shook my head. I wondered if they would turn around and notice me. My arms were full of dresses stacked up to my shoulder, spilling over the side of my elbow and onto the floor.

The snide remarks whirled around inside my head. A few years ago, I would have jumped in and defended the honor of my beloved clothing store. I would have explained that I was holding a thousand dollars' worth of designer dresses that would total fewer than fifty dollars at the register.

Nah, it wasn't worth it.

....

I took a deep breath and smiled as I looked at the outfit I had just found. My favorite brand at 90 percent off. I was fine.

Pastor Andrew Arndt said this a couple of weeks ago in a service: "You don't need to justify your existence to anyone."

And it struck a nerve with me.

How many people had I tried to justify my value to? My decisions to? My very existence to?

A lot of people.

As if them approving of my decisions made me somehow more correct. As if them affirming me gave me more value. Or perhaps it made my self-perceived failures a little more palatable.

But it had become tiring.

As my mom says, there's only so much energy that you have. You can spend it trying to convince random people of your perspective, of your voice, or you can put that energy toward living your life. And being a voice.

And Bishop Jakes has perhaps the best quote on this—given in a TV interview when asked how he responded to all of the people who criticized him. He said that a giraffe and a turtle can share the same space, but only if the giraffe doesn't try to stoop down to the same viewpoint as the turtle.[24]

....

Bam!

Perhaps that is part of finding your voice—being comfortable enough in who you are that you don't have to convince every passerby of your viewpoint. That you don't need affirmation to keep speaking. That you can just walk along in what you're meant to do and focus your energy on that.

I'd like to get so comfortable in my own skin to where I don't feel a need to defend every action or decision to acquaintances or strangers. Or even to friends. I'm getting there.

In the meantime, I know I have to walk through a bit of uncomfortable. A bit of pulling myself together and keeping going when the voices around me say something different. I'm making progress.

And maybe that's why I didn't respond. Maybe those affirmations I had been hearing finally dug in somewhere beneath the shallow surface of my journal-writing hopeful messages.

Maybe they had burrowed in deeper to my lingering unconscious and formed a subtle mantra of "I'm okay. I don't need to defend everything. My decisions are okay. My life is okay . . . Now back off, lady, so I can get to the rest of the dresses."

Okay, that last part was clearly not the words of any famous speakers. But I think my mom would have approved.

....

```
┌─────────────────────────────────────────────┐
│                                               │
│         PERSONAL NOTES                         │
│                                               │
│   SUBJECT  The British Conundrum              │
│   YEAR     Present Day                         │
│                                               │
└─────────────────────────────────────────────┘
```

I was being interviewed for a radio talk show awhile back—a radio show in the UK, no less—and the interviewer was having quite a time. I had just published a book targeted to the young singles market, and I was on the PR circuit promoting it. We talked about all sorts of things during the interview. We covered spirituality, beauty, society in general, and I'm sure there was a conversation about Cheetos and Nutella thrown in.

Then the interviewer threw this one at me from left field: "Do you scare guys? Are guys scared of you?" Except that he was British, and it came across as, "Do you scaeh guys? Ah they scaehd of you?"—making it sound even more profound and ominous. He continued, "You wrote a book that talked about dating . . . do you scaeh them?"

I hadn't thought about that one. Not quite in that way. I stammered something like, "Hmmm . . . I hope not," and awkwardly continued. Of course, later I thought of a million clever things to say, like:

> *I hope so—let's filter out the scared ones.*
> *Is scared the new sexy? The new black? It isn't really my thing.*
> *Well, it's a little late now, isn't it? Quick, let's hide all of the books*
>   *and make the tweens sign confidentiality agreements.*

In the Scarlet Pimpernel,
   he calls this
      "carriage wit"

· 45 ·

I went home that night, and I thought about it. And I worried about it more than a bit . . . I wrote things—did that scare guys?

I talked to one of my guy friends about it over pizza. He confirmed my worst suspicion. He said that it did indeed intimidate some guys when girls wrote books or blogs. I figured I could cross him off my list as a potential Valentine date, but he did pick up the tab for the pizza. Perhaps I had scared him into it. I suppose there were upsides.

I kept thinking about it—had I chosen the wrong life path? Were people really scared of me because I had chosen one hobby over another? That idea felt bizarre.

A short time later, I ran into a similar sentiment when I stumbled into online dating. I say stumbled, because God knows I didn't enter into it gracefully. I tend to do things full-force and yet guardedly. I'm an uncertain hurricane, that's what I am. So when I filled out my first online profile, it was a doozy. I was pretty happy with my result.

uncertaincane — it's a thing

I went to dinner with two of my close (married) friends. The guy had heard of my online dating saga and was feeling rather protective. And nosy. Mostly nosy. He pulled out his smartphone and found my profile.

"Hmmm . . . well . . . hmm . . . humph!"
(Not what a girl wants to hear.)
"What is it?" I asked. "What's wrong with my profile?"
"Well," he said, "it looks okay. It's just . . . "
"What? Just what?"

. . . .

He paused.

"It's just your profile has some red flags . . . "

My eyebrows rose, and I leaned forward. Was it the picture of me hugging a bag of cacao beans? Because I did love chocolate a little too much.

"It has red flags of intelligence. Not all guys want to date a girl who sounds intelligent. The thought of being with an intelligent or successful girl for decades sounds exhausting. They may not write to you."

He was dead serious.

Red flags. I apparently had red flags of intelligence.

Suddenly the British interview came back to my mind with startling clarity. And I realized that all of it came down to me asking one single question:

"So?"

The question continued, "So? So what? If guys are scared of you, what are you going to do now? What will you change? Who will you become? What echo will you be bound by? How far will you go to become something else?"

And then I figured out the real answer to the radio interviewer's question and mine. The answer was that all he said might be true, but it didn't

. . . .

really matter. I was being me—me at the core of my being. And if three billion guys were put off by that, then maybe I would stumble across one who wasn't.

This "So?" question goes way, way beyond the radio interview or anything related to dating. I have at least one chance encounter per week where someone disapproves of what I do or who I am. And it won't stop. There will always be someone who doesn't care for the way I do things.

If I work from sunup until sundown, someone will say I'm not trying hard enough. If I dress with every sense of style and fashion, then someone will say I'm not pretty enough. If I spray myself down with fake tan to fit in at the beach, then it will end in disaster, and people will call me embarrassing nicknames for a year. This I can tell you from experience.

It will happen.

Someone will not like who I am or who you are. They will voice disapproval of our dreams, our personalities, or our opinions.

And at each of those times, we have the opportunity to stop and ask ourselves, "So? Who will I become? What echo will I be bound by? How far will I go to become something else?" And then we can answer, "You know what? It's okay; I'm being true to myself, and I'm good with that. I think I'll keep speaking my voice."

So in the end, I decided I would be like the guys who answered correctly

....

in the Solomon Asch experiment; I would pull myself together and stick to my guns and live from my truth, even though it was uncomfortable. I would shrug off the negative comments as Paul and Barnabas had, and I would be a voice.

Because the other option was switching to someone who wasn't me for the chance of being approved by someone who was looking for someone besides me. And that option wasn't only a confusingly long sentence, it wasn't really an option at all. So I figured I'd take my chances being me. The real me.

And besides that, anyone who was that scared off by a book to help single girls probably needed to grow a set anyway. I wish I would have said that on air. I'm pretty sure the UK wouldn't have minded. I know darn sure Lilac and Magenta would have loved it.

....

PART II

CHANGING THE ECHO

....

ECHO [EK-OH]

...

3. (verb)
(of a sound) be repeated or reverberate after the original sound has stopped.

...

"their footsteps echoed on the metal catwalks"

4. (noun)
A lingering trace or effect.

PERSONAL NOTES

SUBJECT *The Green Sweatpants*

YEAR *Not Too Long Ago*

"Kinda . . . so I was wondering . . . " He paused and shifted his weight. "Yes?" I grinned and turned my attention toward him. "You always used to wear such stylish clothes. Couldn't you wear something a little cuter . . . more fitted . . . tighter?"

Most of the blood drained from my face, and my hands went ice cold. I knew if I caught my reflection in a mirror at that very moment that it would be an ashen gray. And it wouldn't be cute like in the vampire movies.

Part of me wanted to be indignant: "Dude . . . we're camping," I wanted to yell. "Caaaaaam-piiiiing. Are you kidding me? Are you freaking kidding me?"

Yes, the confident me raged at him.

But somewhere inside, a scared little girl stumbled to gain footing and tried to find a solid wall to brace her hand against.

Perhaps it shouldn't have affected me as much as it did. He had probably

. . . .

been right to a point, and I should have let it go. But it was one phrase in a long line of prose that I had heard from others before. I wasn't exactly known for the most normal wardrobe choices growing up, and words hit harder when we're already a little tender from the previous punch.

I guess my camping fashion hadn't quite hit the mark. That was why he had been acting weird. We didn't last much longer after that. But the words from the previous half-decades did. Word after sentence after paragraph. All of them.

They echoed long after everyone had gone. I kept them around and let them play on repeat when the nights were dark and I was alone. I made them into soft, semi-comforting blankets of excuses and wrapped myself in them whenever I was unsure about the world.

Months passed, and I still heard them.

They echoed into each new relationship.

I didn't know it then, but I was creating what I wanted least. I had been filling in where they had stopped. Everyone had left, and I had continued their voices, ruminating on the words and swishing them back and forth in the watery caverns of my mind. I had hated the words, yet I was taking them with me.

It would take me years to realize what was happening and a random science journal article to bring all of the pieces together.

But when all of the pieces came together, it changed my mind.

....

RESEARCH NOTES

SUBJECT *The Girl Who Remembers Everything*

YEAR *December 19, 1981*

Interview: Jill

Subject: The day of December 19, 1981

Notes: It was a Saturday. Jill went shopping in Beverly Hills. She went to see her friend that afternoon who had just made the cheerleading squad. And that night she went out with Harry.

She wore a gray turtleneck sweater. Later they picked up some ice cream.[1]

December 19, 1981—What made the day so special that Jill would remember it?

Nothing. Absolutely nothing.

Jill remembers every day.

....

For most of us, the mundane fades from our minds. The trivial things that happen throughout the day get categorized as unimportant and are swept away from our minds, as with the tide of the sea. We don't need to remember how many cups of coffee we had for dinner three years ago, and so we simply don't.

But what if we never forgot those mundane things from each day? What if tiny events were documented and filed away as if they were extremely important? Just imagine if you could relive your memories with as much emotion as if they happened yesterday. That's what life is like for Jill Price.

As far as she can think back, Jill can recall in small detail the events from every day of her waking life. Name a previous date, and she will tell you what day of the week it fell on. She can remember what significant national events happened *and* what personal *un*eventful things happened at that time. Jill can pull pictures and stories like a rolodex from her mind.

She lets us inside her head for a moment in her book *The Woman Who Can't Forget.*

> As I grew up and more and more memories were stored in my brain, more and more of them flashed through my mind in this endless barrage, and I became a prisoner to my memory . . . My mother would tell me not to dwell on things so much, and I'd try to explain that I wasn't dwelling, that the memories just flooded my mind.[2]

This made it particularly difficult for Jill when negative events would happen, because they all stuck in her mind.

> I think my mother's obsession about my weight was inspired by a pediatrician I went to when I was seven. He commented about my "baby fat," and from then on, she was on the case, putting me on a diet and watching my weight like a hawk . . . Though I took my mother's comments very much to heart, my way of dealing with her admonitions was to rebel.[3]

Jill tells in great detail the sometimes-debilitating effects of having to remember everything. She has a hard time letting go of the simplest of things, because they all have an emotional connection. The painful memories never fade and the vivid memories cause her to cling tightly to nostalgic items.

Doll from childhood? Keep. Napkin from dinner? Keep. She has boxes and boxes of all her childhood toys she saved.[4]

Jill's condition is so rare that it was previously undiagnosed by doctors. It's called hyperthymesia, and it's characterized by having a biographical memory of sorts.[5]

Reading through her story, I thought it sounded exhausting trying to deal with all those thoughts.

For the rest of us, our brains function differently. As odd as it sounds, we are blessed with the ability to forget.

....

But certain things do stick around in our lives. If anything life-altering, scary, or unusual happens, our brains flag it to remember it later. That's why you can probably recall your first date (not that it was unusual, necessarily, just special to you) or where you were when a tragedy occurred.[6]

And there are other times when we consciously or unconsciously take people's words and give them extra importance in our lives. Comments can become filed away and echo forward in our lives to have a powerful influence over us. We may even remember them as clearly as Jill remembered everything.

Recently I was speaking at a conference, and I saw a prime example of how a fifteen-year-old girl did this very thing.

```
SCIENCE NOTES

Why do we remember some things in detail like it
was yesterday? Scientists believe this is because
when our emotions are heightened because of scary,
exciting, or important happenings, our brains flood
with epinephrine and cortisol, allowing a sort of
Polaroid snapshot to happen. It's the brain's way
of saying, "Hey! This is important! File this away
for later."[7]
```

PERSONAL NOTES

SUBJECT The Girl at the Conference

YEAR Not Too Long Ago

We think we've gone along our way and left the past behind. And then we see we've carried with us echoes in our minds.

"How many of you remember a comment that someone made about your looks a month ago?" I watched as hands went up all around the room. "How about a year ago?" A few of the hands went down. "Five years ago? Ten?"

Quite a few of the hands went down then; all of the tweens were barely in diapers ten years before. But the adult hands stayed up, and we took the question further. Many of them had memories of comments made to them when they were youngsters decades ago.

Their memories weren't just straight-lined, sterile, and unemotional though. I watched the women's faces. People nodded forcefully. I watched eyebrows squinch up and faces wince. I think I lost a few there as they drifted off into nostalgia. Hardly anyone smiled. Apparently nostalgia wasn't a fun place to be.

....

I knew if I walked around and asked each of them, they could tell me stories with vivid imagery and startling clarity.

"Who wants to share a comment that you think has changed you?"

A girl of no more than fifteen raised her hand.

"My mom called me a slut from the time I was, I don't know, five or so. She always called me names like that. After a while, I thought, well, if that's what she says, then that must be what I am. And so I guess I was."

Silence. The room itself held its breath. There wasn't anything funny anymore. I have no memory of anything said after that.

Maybe nothing was.

PERSONAL NOTES

SUBJECT _Take It to Heart_

YEAR _Not Too Long Ago_

They call it "taking things to heart," this thing we do. It means we take something seriously. We believe it. We hear it, pull it in, and tell ourselves that it deserves a space of importance in our minds. We concentrate on it.

Good or bad, those things become the words and pictures replaying in our minds. Some people even refer to it as the audiotape in their heads. (And those people were born before 1990 and have actually seen an audiotape.)

We take things to heart that we hear, and we carry them with us until we can recite them with resounding clarity and assuredness.

Those words the fifteen-year-old girl heard? She had taken them to heart. They had stuck with her. And those words I had been holding on to? They had been causing more of an effect than I had realized.

Years later, a young researcher named Tal Harmelech opened my eyes to what had been happening. The echo of the words I had been imagining? It had been real.

....

```
┌─────────────────────────────────────────────────┐
│                                                   │
│              RESEARCH NOTES                       │
│                                                   │
│   SUBJECT  Trace Echoes                           │
│   YEAR     2013                                   │
│                                                   │
└─────────────────────────────────────────────────┘
```

We know instinctively that things replay in our minds. The phrases are everywhere.

> *I can't get you out of my head.*
> *I can't get it off my mind.*
> *This is keeping me up at night.*
> *Your words are echoing in my head.*

We know that it happens, but we don't really see it happening.

Or we didn't.

Until now.

Enter Tal Harmelech.

....

The brain doesn't rest when the body does. It simply switches forms of activity. But one thing had always puzzled scientists when they viewed

....

brain activity. There were times when the brain would have periods of spontaneous activity when the body was resting. And the scientists wondered, *What was going on with that?*

Tal Harmelech thought it might be echoes of what had happened earlier, so her newest research centered on what people thought intentionally about and concentrated on.

In part of her research study, Harmelech told volunteers to think about starting a new project. She had them fully concentrate on it. These thoughts triggered a part of the brain called the dorsal anterior cingulate cortex, which is used in decision-making.[8]

Then Harmelech and her team scanned people's brains with fMRI machines, and the screens lit up like the Fourth of July. (If the Fourth of July had fireworks that were shaped like a person's cortex, that is.)[9]

SCIENCE NOTES:

fMRI-functional magnetic resonance imaging-machines scan the brain to detect changes in blood flow and oxygenation level in different regions of the brain. Blood flow is linked to neural (brain cell) activity. So by scanning the brain with fMRI machines, scientists can tell which parts of the brain are active.[10]

. . . .

Harmelech came back six minutes after the volunteers stopped concentrating and scanned again. One full day later, Harmelech scanned their brains a third time. What she found was surprising and a little scary.

There were traces in the brain twenty-four hours later of what the person had thought about the day before.[11]

"The patterns of firing neurons observed during the concentration task could still be seen when the brain was in its resting state—though they had not been active before the task."[12]

This was more than just seeing a passing thought flicker on an fMRI screen. She could see what type of things they had thought about twenty-four hours before. And those traces were stronger twenty-four hours later than just after the person thought about it.

Science journalist Douglas Heaven called this "echoes in the brain."[13]

Their thoughts had echoed forward.

How did this happen? A little mix of ~~Play-Doh and baling wire.~~ No!

I Meant plasticity and Hebbian wiring!

```
┌─────────────────────────────────────────────┐
│ ┌─────────────────────────────────────────┐ │
│ │                                         │ │
│ │        RESEARCH  NOTES                  │ │
│ │                                         │ │
│ │   SUBJECT   Hebbian Wiring              │ │
│ │   YEAR      Present Day                 │ │
│ │                                         │ │
│ └─────────────────────────────────────────┘ │
└─────────────────────────────────────────────┘
```

Our brains are ever-changing and ever-learning. It's a concept called plasticity, although I always picture Play-Doh when I hear that word. (And then I always think of salty foods, for obvious reasons.)

Picture yourself holding Play-Doh and turning it over in your hands. It's moldable and shapeable. And unless it's been left out in the sun or put in the microwave (looks awkwardly to side), it's pretty soft. That's the concept of what plasticity means. It means our brains are moldable and are able to change throughout life. We can learn new ways of doing things.

It means that the way we think today will change our brains for tomorrow, and the things we concentrate on now will echo forward into our futures.

One way is through Hebbian learning.[14]

If we hear two ideas together (such as "Amy" and "intelligent"), then those neurons are "firing" together at the same time. And when we

....

connect two ideas together over and over, those neurons in our brain actually start wiring themselves together.

The same thing happens with negative thoughts. If you concentrate on negative things over and over, then your brain cells start wiring to view the world in that way. It becomes easier and easier to be negative. The neurons that fire together, wire together.

SCIENCE-Y QUOTE
"The general idea is an old one, that any two cells or systems of cells that are repeatedly active at the same time will tend to become 'associated', so that activity in one facilitates activity in the other."[15]

Axon Terminal
Myelin Sheath
Cell Body
Dendrite
Mitochondria
Nucleus

I like the visual of a herd of cattle walking across a field, day after day. After a while, a trail starts to form across the field, and the cattle start following a pattern of walking down that path. Those are like the paths that form in our minds. When we think certain thoughts over and over, we're creating pathways of sorts in our brain. As the neurons "wire" together, it forms a pattern of thinking.

What does this mean? It means if someone speaks words to you and you take them to heart and meditate on them over and over, your brain starts wiring to think that way. The more you concentrate on it, the easier it is for you to believe it.

....

Even if that person has left and gone, if you meditate on it, it will echo forward into your future. It will affect how you act and who you become.

It's more than just hocus-pocus-throw-some-magic-unicorn-dust-in-the-air-and-wish-upon-a-star positive thinking. (Although if you do find unicorn dust, that would probably be a good use for it.) It's what happens in our minds when we intentionally focus our mind, energy, and attention toward something over and over. It changes the way our brains work.

The positive, healthy thoughts build on one another. The negative thoughts do as well. They echo.

The good news? You can unwire your brain. Or I should say, rewire your brain. Good grief, don't unwire it.

Dr. Caroline Leaf explains it this way in her book *Switch on Your Brain:* "Neuroplasticity can operate for us as well as against us, because whatever we think about most will grow."[16]

You can rewire the way you think about life and what you believe about yourself. It does take time, but you can replace those words and thoughts. The things you concentrate on and take to heart, you can change them.

> "As a single footstep will not make a path on the earth, so a single thought will not make a pathway in the mind. To make a deep physical path, we must walk again and again. To make a deep mental path, we must think over and over the kind of thoughts we wish to dominate our lives."[17]
>
> Wilferd Peterson

RESEARCH NOTES

SUBJECT _Trace Echoes - My Reaction_

YEAR _Present Day_

I remember reading about Tal Harmelech's Hebbian learning study for the first time and it stopping me cold in my mental cow-across-the-field tracks. It explained so much about the way that I saw myself. I knew that when negative things had been spoken to me, I had gone home and thought about them over and over. And over and over.

And each time I had gone through any form of rejection, I had absorbed the full weight of its impact. I would lie awake for hours questioning, blaming, and giving my brain plenty of ammunition for future worry sessions.

It had worked its way into the core of my being—past the sentences hurled at me hanging out in my short-term memory. It had found its way into the subtle corners of my life.

Even if those negative things weren't true, I was concentrating on them so much that they had become true in my mind. I was living in a way as if it were true.

Was it possible for the brain to habitually think something for so long that it did not even recognize the truth in front of it? Was that what I had been doing?

....

```
┌─────────────────────────────────────────────┐
│  ┌───────────────────────────────────────┐  │
│  │                                         │  │
│  │        RESEARCH  NOTES                  │  │
│  │                                         │  │
│  │   SUBJECT  Phantom Pain                 │  │
│  │   YEAR     2014                         │  │
│  │                                         │  │
│  └───────────────────────────────────────┘  │
└─────────────────────────────────────────────┘
```

Stephen Sumner never thought he would be in the middle of Cambodia with a stack of mirrors tied to the back of a bicycle. But there he was, in the Spean Tomneap village in the Battambang province of northwestern Cambodia.

Riding a bicycle and carrying mirrors.

Author Srinath Perur reported as he rode along with Sumner:

> Stephen, 53, is a brawny Canadian with an ebullient, even boisterous, manner. This is his third time here in as many years. He rides around on a longtail bicycle with a stack of lightweight mirrors behind the saddle, going to villages, hospitals and physical rehabilitation centres looking for people who have lost their limbs.
>
> Just as the pain of war lingers long after it is over, so an amputee's pain can persist long after the limb has gone. It can be harrowing and difficult to treat with medication or surgery. Stephen helps people deal with their phantom pain, and he does it with mirrors.

. . . .

· 14 ·

We're in Spean Tomneap village in the Battambang province of north-western Cambodia—the most heavily mined region in one of the most heavily mined countries in the world. We've driven up along a mud road lined by fields and houses surrounded by tangled greenery. Stephen is perched on the landing near the staircase of a weathered wooden house on stilts. Chickens scurry about. A few onlookers gather.

In front of Stephen on an upturned pail sits Ven Phath, a soft-spoken, middle-aged father of five. His left trouser leg is rolled up to reveal a stump below the knee, the result of stepping on a mine in 1983. A plasticky prosthetic leg lies beside him.

....

Ven Phath still experiences pain in his missing
foot, and Stephen is showing him how to position a
mirror against the inside of his left leg, so the
reflection of the right makes it look like both
are still intact. "Look. Move. Imagine," Stephen
instructs through an interpreter.

After a couple of minutes of watching his virtual
left foot moving, as if revving an imaginary
accelerator, Ven Phath smiles and looks up. He
says he feels better already. "Tell him," Stephen
says to the interpreter, "if you do this twice a
day, ten minutes per session, for five weeks, then
chhub chhue." Pain stop.[18]

As Stephen Sumner found, some amputees feel as if they are moving or touching their limb that is gone, a phenomenon that has become known as having a "phantom limb."[19] An estimated 50 to 80 percent of amputees experience pain in their phantom limb, and that pain is often excruciating.[20] Many patients say they can even move their phantom limbs. And just as intriguing is that equal numbers say that their phantom limb is paralyzed.[21]

An arm or leg that they no longer have is still there—but paralyzed.

Researchers Ramachandran and Altschuler theorized that this was at least partly from Hebbian learning. That the initial paralysis became "stamped" in the brain as a form of "learned paralysis"—which then carried over into the phantom.[22]

The brain had wired itself to believe that the arm or leg was paralyzed, even after that was no longer true. One strategy to treat this is to rewire the brain with mirror box therapy.

A mirror box is a box with a, um . . . mirror. The box is split down the middle with a mirror with a hole on one side for the amputee to insert his or her arm. They then look at the box from an angle, so that it looks as if they have two good arms.

Once the brain sees both arms moving, it sends a signal to say, "Hey, everything's moving again! We're all good here, everyone calm down."

SCIENCE NOTES:

This phenomenon appears to happen more often if the arm had been paralyzed from a peripheral nerve lesion or injury before the amputation.[23]

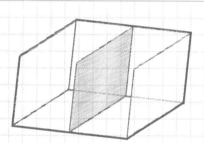

Whatever position the arm had been stuck in before, it remained after, as if "stuck in cement" or "frozen in a block of ice."[24]

Okay, that's an oversimplification, but a sort of rewiring in the brain does occur to say that the arm is no longer paralyzed.

And for Stephen at least, using a mirror worked swimmingly for his own phantom leg. He himself is an amputee and had suffered with phantom pains for years.

....

"Everything was good," he said. "But my leg that's not there was killing me."[25]

As Perur reported, "Stephen used the mirror for two weeks, then stopped because the pain had not returned. About a year and a half later, he felt the pain again, and this time he stayed the course for the full five weeks. He hasn't had phantom pain for over four years. 'It's gone now,' he says. 'It's gone because I treated myself with a mirror.'"[26]

....

Scientists and doctors debate both the effectiveness of the mirror box treatment in different situations and the brain mechanisms by which any sort of cure could occur. One thing that's clear is, our brain has powerful capabilities of forming learned connections.

It can cause an arm to be paralyzed that isn't there.

And it can tell someone they're not enough when they're amazing.

But what gives me hope is that with the right mirror, it can also recognize truth and change.

....

PERSONAL NOTES

SUBJECT *Recognition: The Subtle Things*
YEAR *Not Too Long Ago*

The value is not in the finding or in the convenience. It is in the recognition.

"I want to come over and hang out," my friend Christina said. "I want to hear about your day."

"You can't. You simply can't," I countered. "I don't think you know what I'm like today. It hasn't been a good day. I'm halfway through a carton of ice cream. I'm not a nice person right now. Really. I don't even like me right now. I'm a jerk tonight."

"I don't care. That's why I want to come over. I'm not friends with your happy emotion, silly. I'm friends with you. It's my pleasure to come hang out with you."

The words registered, but then again, they didn't. This person offered friendship with no bartering. My friend said my worth was something other than my ability to dish out gifts and my offerings of gratitude and advisement. My friend had seen my worst and wanted to hang out with me.

....

And I realized something . . .

I was surprised.

....

It's not always the obvious that gets you. Not the voice in your head that says you're horrible. Not the words yelled and hurled at you.

Sometimes it's the subtle, underlying rhythm you didn't know was there. The thoughts and ideas that buried themselves deep when you were distracted with other notions. Slowly, bit by bit. The situations, side comments, the love and lack of it served to you in tiny, bite-sized pieces. And at some point along the way, they burrowed in and softly started echoing in your life.

Sometimes it's the subtle that gets you.

My friend Kristian echoed the sentiment a few weeks later.

"Kinda, I think you're confident, but I don't think you really get who you are. I don't think you've really gotten your identity yet. And when you get it, you're going to walk with a new light and confidence. You're going to be a different person. When you really get it. When you *really* see it. You don't yet, but one day you will."

What she didn't realize was that she was part of the mirror helping me to recognize, helping me to really get it.

And once you recognize it, you can begin.

....

PERSONAL NOTES

SUBJECT _Creating Tomorrow Today_

YEAR _Present Day_

The old saying is that we start fresh and new every morning. It's not quite that simple. Yes, the things from yesterday affect today. But the good news is, the things we think on today will affect us tomorrow.

Today we help to create our tomorrow.

It builds on itself. The phrase "renew your mind daily" took on a new meaning after reading those studies. The meditations of our minds will carry over. Every time we choose to concentrate on a positive, encouraging word instead of a discouraging one, we make it easier to do so tomorrow. We set the stage for how our brains behave in the future.

First, we have to be aware of the things we're thinking and telling ourselves. Some writers call this capturing your thoughts. Others call it gathering thoughts, reflection, or even just recognition, as I had labeled it with the subtle things in my life.

The point is, we have to first take a moment to stop and listen to what's being echoed forward. I know, I know, stopping and listening is tough with a busy life, but it's important.

Challenge: Write down one word or phrase (or idea) echoing in your mind and soul that isn't the truth. (It shouldn't be there.)

I teach business classes at a local university, and I often have my students keep a thought journal for a week, just to see what things keep going through their minds. I've done this myself as well. It's very enlightening to see internal thoughts written down on a page.

Be aware of what's echoing inside. If something doesn't fit the truth of your identity—or what truth you're moving toward—it's time to let it go. If you become aware of a negative pattern of thinking, don't keep meditating on it. Start replacing it in your mind with what the truth is. The truth gives us freedom to no longer be bound by the negative echoes of the past.

I'm not saying you can't have a bad day. I'm saying what you continually concentrate on will subtly affect you.

If you really want to change the things that have been echoing forward, you have to recognize what is going on with your thoughts and intentionally work to change them. Start moving the cows across the field in a new direction.

Day after day, your brain will form new connections and your emotions will become even healthier.

The crazy part is, if you keep doing this, you'll start to notice which negative things in the environment are affecting you, and you won't be so casual about allowing them around anymore.

You'll look back at the end of a year and realize how much your brain has changed.

Day after day, echo upon echo, the amazing can happen.

....

WHICH WOLF YOU FEED

Many years ago, a young Cherokee boy came to his grandfather, hurt and angry about a friend who had betrayed him. His grandfather listened patiently to the boy's story, watching his hands clench and eyes brighten with tears.

When the boy finished, the grandfather slowly sat down and looked at the boy kindly. "I, too, have had many injustices done to me, sometimes at the hands of my friends. It is at those times, I feel that a fight is going on inside of me. A fight between two wolves.

"One wolf wants nothing but revenge. He is angry and unfeeling. He wants war and greed and to tear apart anything that stands in his path. He is filled with pride and arrogance, selfishness and resentment.

"The other wolf fights him. The wolf is kind and forgiving. He calmly responds, is brave, and has no malice. He is filled with grace and compassion and reaches out in peace to his enemies. I feel conflicted many times because this war between the two wolves is waging inside of me."

The grandson nodded in understanding. "But, Grandfather, which wolf wins the fight?"

The grandfather paused and spoke quietly. "Whichever one I feed."

Old Native American story that has been retold many different ways over the years.[27]

PERSONAL NOTES

SUBJECT _Losing Me, Finding Me_

YEAR _Present Day_

I have to be honest here—something unexpected happened when I started to intentionally focus on thinking healthier thoughts.

I lost something, and maybe even someone, and I didn't like it.

You lose someone when you recognize and rewire; when you change the echo. You lose your excuses. You lose the comfortable person you were, and I thought I would be thrilled with that.

I was surprised that I felt the need to mourn her—that person I lost. I never expected that.

A part of me missed her.

She was my "yeah but" that I could say after each compliment. She was the "ah, that's why" to every rejection.

She was the one who built safe walls of protection against real vulnerability. She dismissed and downplayed and distanced herself right into a zone of safety.

....

Safety.

Safety.

Changing might have been healthier, but it was a scary thought, this stepping outside of my normal pattern and risking rejection.

And this thought was the kicker that scared me the most: *If I throw away all of my excuses and still am not good enough . . . what then?*

Many of us deal with this. We don't want mirrors of truth held up in front of us because the images we've created of who we are feel safe and comforting.

It may seem easier to call on a supposedly fatal flaw for justification than to step into a new and uncomfortable realm of living. But we were meant for more than that.

We were meant to live in truth and freedom. And getting to freedom isn't always comfortable. I'm not even sure that living in it is. But it's a heck of a lot better than staying where we are because we're afraid to change or afraid of the real version of ourselves.

So we have to make choices.

One of mine showed up in a green box with a ribbon on it.

FAMOUS Quote
"The time came when the risk to remain tight in the bud, was more painful than the risk that it took to blossom."[28]

. . . .

LAB JOURNAL

Letting all of it go
Piece by piece it's
    Coming out slow
Fish hooks with barbed ends
Jagged tears on fleshy skin
And I never knew this process
would be so complicated and drawn-out,
I shed the first layer
    Like winter scarves
Tossed it aside and relinquished the part
And danced a small dance at my
  -obvious- victory
But now I'm finding you in places
I didn't even know I had let you in
Deeper layers beneath my skin
And suddenly I don't feel like
Such a victor anymore
And I wonder how long all of this will take
Pulling out the pieces of the
Image I made
And I wonder who I will be
By the time I get there

. . . .

PERSONAL NOTES

SUBJECT _The Green Box_

YEAR _Present Day_

I sat there staring at the box in my hands—green with a red ribbon strapped across the top. It had been picked up at an after-Christmas sale at a crazy-good discount. I had been so excited to find the box then. But I wasn't now. I slowly shifted the box back and forth from one hand to the other and blinked rapidly as tears threatened. I was lost in thought.

I slowly removed the lid and peered inside. Letters. A Ziploc bag of flower petals. A few other trinkets. The list went on and on. I inhaled sharply as I looked at the items. What was all of this doing here? I didn't remember keeping so many of these things. I had slowly collected them, one at a time. Then after the breakup, I had pulled all of the "couple" pictures down, packed everything in a box, and shoved it as far back as I could into my closet. I just hadn't wanted to deal with it at the time. I still didn't.

But a lot of things had become clear to me that week. I didn't yet know where my life would take me, and I didn't know where the next step would be or where the man I needed to meet was. But I knew where all of those things weren't. And I knew where the guy wasn't. For one, he wasn't in all of those memories that I had kept tucked away. And he

. . . .

wasn't in that box. He was probably much too tall to fit, for one thing.

And my future wasn't in that box. Sometimes things go in stages. And grief is a process, not a step. But so is moving on.

And I had moved on—or so I had thought. But I realized that a small part of me was tied to those memories. My mind would drift back and reminisce. My brain would go to "what-ifs" and "if-thens." And a tiny part of my soul still gazed back and sighed.

They say in skiing that if you want to turn left or right, the easiest way to do it is to look in that direction. Well, how was I supposed to go forward . . . if I kept looking back? If I kept dwelling on it? If I kept thinking about it all the time? I knew then that in my heart of hearts, it was time to move on. It was time to get healthy. For real this time.

As I sat there holding the box, my breath quickened. I felt like those people on the *Hoarders* show where the therapist tries to make them throw away the cat figurine and the hoarder panics. And you watch the show and think, *Good grief—it's not like it's a real cat or anything.* But still the hoarder starts crying or throws a fit, and it makes for great television.

I looked at the box in my hands—it was just a box of old trinkets. So why was it so hard? One phrase gently sounded in the back of my mind. *This isn't the best thing that will happen to you. This isn't the best.*

I sat there, stunned. Did I really believe that? Maybe I was holding on because somewhere, deep inside, I questioned if I would ever find

. . . .

someone else or find something better. Somewhere a small voice of doubt had been whispering over and over, *You'll probably be fine, but maybe, just maybe, this is all there is. This is the best that will happen. And it's already done, so hold on tight. Just hold on tight.*

Wow. Was that what had been echoing in my thoughts? Is that what I had allowed myself to believe? I didn't like where those thoughts were going at all. I really did believe there was something better. I really did believe that better things would come. Or I was starting to believe it.

And I knew what I had to do.

I knew where my future wasn't. And it wasn't in that box. It wasn't in looking in my past. And it wasn't in those old thoughts and emotions that were apparently still hovering around. Yep, I knew what I had to do.

I called a girlfriend or two and told them we needed to dispose of a few things, and I asked if I could borrow their fire pit. I requested that they have chocolate handy. They didn't even ask. They knew.

It was time to cut a few soul ties and move on to a healthier place. After all, it's hard to run forward when you're looking back. And it's hard to reach your future destiny when you're still holding on to the negativity of the past.

When you're still living someone else's words that have been spoken about you.

. . . .

It was time to start focusing on who I was meant to be and begin rewriting the words and thoughts that had been echoing in my mind.

I sat and watched as the papers curled up and turned black within the flames. I thought about all that I had been through those last few years—how much I had grown and how excited I was to begin the next chapter of my life. I dropped the last letter in and watched it all slowly shrink and disappear.

It was time to start a new echo.

I reminisced. I cried. I wiped the tears. And I let it go.

Let me look straight ahead, unwavering. Let me walk through this uncomfortable path and go where I need to go.

Challenge: take what you wrote earlier. Write the truth here to replace it with. Write who you are at your core and who you know you can be. Start changing your echo.

P.S. Do with that first list what you wish

. . . .

PART III

BREAKING OUT
OF THE DEATH SPIRAL

....

ECHO [EK-OH]

•••

5. (verb)
To be repeated—by or as by an echo.

•••

6. (noun)
Something that is similar to something
that happened or existed before.

PERSONAL NOTES

SUBJECT _Churning Butter on Planes_

YEAR _2011_

Thursday morning, 10:20 a.m. I sat on the plane and stared straight down at my feet.

I'm not up in the air; I'm just on a bus. I'm not up in the air; I'm just on a bus. This is a pothole; I'm just on a bus.

Kawhomp!

The plane dipped momentarily, and my stomach dropped . . . less momentarily. I knew we were just passing through clouds. A nasty round of storms had hit earlier in the afternoon, grounding planes and keeping us sitting in the airport until they passed. Now, strapped into my seat on the plane, I knew three things with absolute certainty:

> We were flying out of Chicago around the storms.
> We were flying through turbulence.
> I was not happy to be on the plane.

This bumpy ride didn't seem to bother anyone quite as much as it did me. My friend Kristian had told me to imagine that I was a superhero flying and dodging clouds. My nurse friends Jennie and Mary had suggested that I take a large array of calming herbal remedies.

....

Some of my other friends had jokingly recommended hard liquor, but I was pretty sure the world wasn't ready for that one. I would be that girl from the movie *Bridesmaids*.

"There is a colonial woman on the wing. There is something they're not telling us. She was out there churning butter. She was CHURNING BUTTER!"

Nope. Couldn't do it.

So there I sat—Benadryl, distracting gossip magazines, and pretty much an entire herbal drugstore on my lap—pretending that I was a superhero flying through clouds. And the plane hit turbulence again.

I was one air pocket away from stuffing my little airplane pillow under my shirt and running around the plane shouting, "I'm in labor! I'm in labor! Land this plane and let me off so I can have this ba-by!" Yes, that would be my shining moment.

I clenched my teeth and looked down at my feet again. *This is what it takes*, I thought. *This is what it takes to get where you want to be.* I opened my journal and looked at all of the things that I had written down dealing with fear. All of them said to fear-not, but none of them said what to do if I still fear-did.

So what if I was still afraid? What was I supposed to do then? I frantically opened up the Bible app on my phone, hit the search function, and typed in Benadryl . . . Nothing. Apparently Jesus didn't have an opinion on that. What was a girl to do?

....

....

Fear is the body's warning that something is wrong—it's a signal for danger. Anxiety is its close cousin and is a feeling of impending doom or that something will be wrong. Some authors say they're almost the same thing, and some distinguish between the two. Either way, they're not emotions you want to have sticking around.

When you initially feel fear, the sympathetic nervous system (SNS) kicks in and regulates things like heart rate and breathing rate. It's what makes your heart beat faster and your pulse quicken. Your first response is largely unconscious—it's automatic.[1]

That meant that there was virtually no chance of me calmly looking around in a chilled-out, cool-kid fashion the first time I experienced turbulence. (Not that I do in normal situations either.)

I went into "fight or flight" mode: when the heart starts frantically pumping blood to the muscles of the legs and preparing them to ruuuuuuun (or kick people).[2]

I didn't know it then, but that was the start of one of the most uncomfortable and challenging learning experiences of my entire life—facing my greatest fear: fear.

It would take a few tips from a contemporary author, a tornado, and an explorer in the early 1900s to figure it all out.

....

RESEARCH NOTES

SUBJECT William Beebe & the Death Spiral

YEAR 1919

In 1919, adventurer William Beebe stumbled across something so puzzling that he almost couldn't believe it. A staggering infantry of millions of deadly Eciton army ants, six lines wide, marching at the pace of two and a half inches a seconds . . . in a giant circle.[3]

William Beebe (the original "Beebs" celebrity, if you will) was an adventurer in the early 1900s. He had quickly become the explorer golden child of America, trekking across countries and writing back to the US in books and newspapers to tell of his vivid and outlandish tales of the outdoors. And wearing some amazing-looking pants in the process.

His work in 1919 brought him to Kartaba, Guyana (Guiana), where he spent hours upon hours huddled in viewing fascination at the interactions of the deadly Eciton army ant communities.

. . . .

And these weren't friendly ants from the Disney cartoons—these ants were vicious. They traveled in tribes and could easily destroy a prey that was a thousand times their size and wipe out an area almost two thousand square yards in a single day. Legend had it that a king had even used them to execute criminals.[4]

This was what William Beebe was dealing with in his ant studies, and he did everything he could to further his research. Once, in an effort to get as close as possible to view an ant nest hanging from the corner of an outhouse, he put a chair in pans of disinfectant to keep the killer ants away. He then balanced atop the chair to avoid a certain death as he observed the ants crawling all around the floor and just above his head. This was a man dedicated to his research.

William Beebe had learned just about every behavior and ritual of the Eciton army ants, but not even he expected to find them marching in a circle. Yet there they were, marching just the same. Beebe traced the path the ants were marching and found that it was almost twelve hundred feet around. This meant it took the ants two and a half hours to trek its circumference. And trek it they did.

Hour after hour they marched, and Beebe watched them.

Scientists would later find that the Eciton ants were blind and often followed the scent of the other ants in their raids. This allowed them to all stay in formation, with the pheromones more concentrated in the very center of the line. They could form a tight group and attack ruthlessly.[5]

....

Somewhere in their genetic wiring though, this deadly efficiency had a glitch. If the line happened to cross itself and form a circle, there became no end, as one ant followed the next into oblivion. It was essentially the lemmings legend in a circle.

Beebe kept watching the ants throughout the day. One by one, the ants became exhausted and bewildered and started dropping. Other ants walked around and over the dead bodies and continued their plight.

Night fell and another day passed, and the ants were still traveling around the circle. By now the ants had circled at least a dozen times, and their numbers had dwindled considerably. Most of the ants had no more life left in them. Beebe kept observing the ants into the next day. Eventually a few broke free—accidentally, confusedly—and stumbled away, bringing a few lone survivors with them.

A once-deadly army reduced to a helpless, confused circle. This phenomenon became known as the death spiral—a death loop.

Author Jeff Wise knows all too well the phenomenon of a death spiral, and not because of his hatred for ants, but because of something else.

1919

"At six o'clock the following morning I started out for a swim, when at the foot of the laboratory steps I saw a swiftly-moving, broad line of army ants on safari, passing through the compound to the beach. I traced them back under the servants' quarters, through two clumps of bamboos to the outhouse.

Later I followed along the column down to the river sand, through a dense mass of underbrush, through a hollow log, up the bank, back through light jungle—to the outhouse again, and on a large fallen log, a few feet beyond the spot where their nest had been, the ends of the circle actually came together!

It was the most astonishing thing, and I had to verify it again and again before I could believe the evidence of my eyes. It was a strong column, six lines wide in many places, and the ants fully believed that they were on their way to a new home, for most were carrying eggs or larvæ, although many had food, including the larvæ of the Painted Nest Wasplets.

For an hour at noon during heavy rain, the column weakened and almost disappeared, but when the sun returned, the lines rejoined, and the revolution of the vicious circle continued."

—William Beebe

[292]

....

• 95 •

RESEARCH NOTES

SUBJECT _The SVOD_

YEAR _Not Too Long Ago_

Author Jeff Wise didn't set out to become an expert on ants, per se, but during his research he realized a striking similarity between the ants' behavior and something he had experienced quite often: anxiety.

Wise made the connection between the ant death circle and his own anxiety after an experience at a party. What started out as normal introvert-at-a-party anxiety suddenly escalated into a full-blown panic attack. The longer he concentrated on his anxiety, the worse it became.

> I realized, to my horror, that something was happening to me that I had no control over—and the more I thought about it, the worse the feeling got. I was in the grips of an anxiety attack. I headed for the door. In the grip of an anxiety attack, I wasn't fearing the party anymore, but the physical sensation of my unease.[7]

It turns out Jeff Wise isn't alone with this type of phenomenon.

My friend Stacy has never heard of Eciton ants or death spirals, but she always talks about something similar—something she calls the Swirling Vortex of Doom.

Stacy explained this phenomenon to me awhile back as we talked about the uncertainty of our futures and anxiously ate bars of chocolate. Stacy said the Swirling Vortex of Doom is when you get wrapped up in your thoughts and fears, and they just take you down. And down. And the more you fear and worry, the more it makes you worry. And you're overwhelmed by it all.

The more you focus on your fears and anxiety, the further down you go. Something so powerful as a human is reduced to anxiety and fear paralysis. It's a Swirling Vortex of Doom. It's a death spiral.

SCIENCE NOTES:

With the Eciton ants, the longer the ants traveled in a circle, the more powerful the pheromones were, so the harder it was to leave.[8] The same thing happens with the Swirling Vortex of Doom—if you focus on your fears, the echoing loop escalates (other names: negative feedback loops).[9]

Yes! A death spiral. I completely related, because it was exactly what I had been feeling for years. I had been stuck in quite a few of them, after all.

Being scared I would die

Fearing I would make a mistake

Being scared to go into new situations

Being fearful that I would mess up and look stupid

. . . .

I had wanted to be brave, but I had been scared. And then I would get scared that I felt scared. And then I would be worried that I was scared that I was scared. Whew. I'm exhausted just writing that.

Here are some of the Swirling Vortices of Doom that my mind had become caught in:

Hears a story on the news about a deadly flu —> Gets nervous —> Worries I may have the deadly flu —> Sneezes —> Worries more —> Googles every symptom of flu —> Freaks out —> Feels worse —> Worries more

Fearful about giving a speech —> Hand starts shaking —> Freaks out because my hand is shaking (Oh no, I'm not supposed to be scared, something is wrong!) —> Freaks out more —> Hand starts shaking more

The fear in each of these situations wouldn't go away, and I became paralyzed. I was in a death spiral.

But there were two obvious problems with this situation.

First, it's hard to go after your dreams while caught in the paralysis of a death spiral. Second, most things we want to do or changes we want to make lie just outside of our comfort zones . . . and we have to pass through fear to get to them.

Think about it—the best adventures and stories and freedoms are beyond your comfort zone. Most things you dream for, go for, or tell stories about are things that initially made you uncomfortable. The best

. . . .

adventures and dreams are the ones with a little bit of fear and risk attached to them.

And the person walking in freedom first has to walk through uncomfortable to get there.

ME —> Fear —> Stuff I want to do, person I want to be

This meant if I were going to keep going after dreams or stepping outside of my comfort zone, I needed to figure out how to deal with this fear thing and not get caught in the death spiral.

ARG.

A possible answer came to me one afternoon while I was doodling fearful ants walking in circles. Because that's what you do when you need important answers.

....

I had had it. Up to here (waves hand back and forth at the top of her head). I was fearful about everything in life. Something was off—I could feel it. There had to be something I could do to make things hunky-dory. (Apparently I start dropping idioms from the South when I'm . . . at my wit's end.)

I grabbed a sheet of paper and started sketching boxes. That's something I do when I'm anxious. I'm a box sketcher. I drew the little Eciton ants going around and around the box and dropping off one by one.

....

Somewhere in my frustration I drew a line down the middle of the page and started a list.

Things that made my fear worse.

Things that made it better.

Not surprisingly, I was doing about 95 percent of only one of those lists. As I looked at the ants and the fear loop again and traced the circles on spiral-bound paper, I realized something. The emotion of fear was only a part of that fear death spiral. The Swirling Vortex of Doom.

I found my Sharpie marker and started charting out a circle and adding what I knew about fear. Things just feel more impactful when written in Sharpie markers. I drew arrows and lines and connected the items together.

One part of the Swirling Vortex of Doom was the initial fear response—

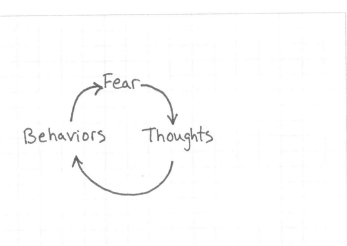

this was the only part I couldn't directly control. You can't choose whether or not you sweat the first time you walk onto a stage or if you scream when someone drops a snake into your lap.

But there was more to the rest of the loop. The listed items fit quite neatly into two other groups:

The thoughts I was thinking
The behaviors I was choosing

I stared at the paper.

WAITAMINUTE.

Hope hit me in the face and refused to be rationalized out of the room. Could fear be changed? Could it be learned and unlearned?

I found part of my answer in bunny rabbits.

. . . .

RESEARCH NOTES

SUBJECT___*Little Albert*___

YEAR___*1920s*___

Little Albert liked bunny rabbits. He was nine months old, and he smiled and giggled when he saw them.[10] He was a kid, after all, and kids are infamously fearless.

Now I don't have kids of my own, but if I did, I imagine they would charge around, painting random objects and sticking things up their noses. And pretty much mirror my childhood experiences with crayons.

That was Little Albert—a kid after my own heart. He was definitely curious.

It was the 1920s, and Little Albert's mom worked at a local hospital. It wasn't long before she was introduced to John Watson and his research assistant at the hospital's lab. Watson advertised that they needed a subject for an experiment, and stories say that Little Albert's mom handed over her son for whatever was to come.[11]

What came was one of the oddest experiments of all time.

Keep in mind that ethics boards for psychology experiments were pretty

. . . .

much nonexistent back then. There was no oversight for Little Albert, and the researchers had just about any freedoms they wanted—all in the name of science, of course. So when it came time to experiment on Little Albert, it was no-holds barred.

The researchers started off by letting Little Albert play with a white rat. Little Albert giggled. He would reach out to it as it scurried around him, begging it to come closer and trying to grasp it with his tiny hands. Like I said, the kid was curious.

The researchers made notes as they watched Little Albert playing with the rat. This was step one.

If only there hadn't been a step two.

The researchers showed Little Albert the white rat again. While this was happening, one of them sneaked up behind Little Albert and struck a large steel bar with a hammer. It clanged loudly. Little Albert heard the loud noise and was terrified and confused. He screamed in fear and cried out.

The researchers tried it again. They put the white rat in front of Little Albert. They clanged the steel bar. Little Albert screamed in terror again.

Soon the sight of anything white and fluffy sent tears coursing down Little Albert's cheeks; rats, fluffy white rabbits, and even Santa's beard brought terror. The scientists had accomplished their mission. Little Albert had learned to fear something that he had once loved—even something that was as harmless as bunny rabbits.

Now he fears even Santa Claus

Little Albert had learned to be afraid.

Watson and his team didn't have time to work with Little Albert any longer, so they sent him home with his mother. When Little Albert left the research lab, he was still terrified of anything white and fluffy. And as far as anyone knows, he always was.[12]

Poor Little Albert. I wanted to go back in time and steal him away and help him learn to like bunny rabbits again.

Something so innocent had become fearful to him. He had learned to fear.

It happens to us as well. Situations happen, and we learn to become afraid. We learn to doubt and worry. It's called *fear conditioning*.[13]

Little Albert might have been conditioned to fear white fluffy things, but I had been conditioned to fear as well.

I mean, bunny rabbits were no problem for me (no thanks to that *Monty Python* movie), but I had learned to fear other things. I feared messing up. I feared looking stupid or failing. I feared being vulnerable. And yes, I feared basically any situation I couldn't control.

But according to research, fears could be unlearned as well; it's called *fear extinction*.[14] If someone had just taken the time with Little Albert after the experiment, he could have learned to enjoy playing with animals again. The fear could have slowly gone away.

Hey - Hebbian learning again?

I looked at my circle sketch again. I was determined to make choices to walk away from my death spiral, beginning with the thoughts I chose. Enter Me versus My Vivid Imagination.

If people can unlearn fear... can our brains learn freedom? Can it become easier to resist conformity??

I read a study...

....

Little Albert Notes - by Watson and Rayner

(At beginning)
"In brief, the infant was confronted suddenly and for the first time successively with a white rat, a rabbit, a dog, a monkey, with masks with and without hair, cotton wool, burning newspapers, etc. . . . At no time did this infant ever show fear in any situation. These experimental records were confirmed by the casual observations of the mother and hospital attendants. No one had ever seen him in a state of fear and rage. The infant practically never cried."

(Starting the experiment)
"One of the two experimenters caused the child to turn its head and fixate her moving hand; the other stationed back of the child, struck the steel bar a sharp blow. The child started violently, his breathing was checked and the arms were raised in a characteristic manner. On the second stimulation the same thing occurred, and in addition the lips began to pucker and tremble. On the third stimulation the child broke into a sudden crying fit. This is the first time an emotional situation in the laboratory has produced any fear or even crying in Albert."

(1 Year 21 Days)
"The rabbit. The animal was placed directly in front of him. It was very quiet. Albert showed no avoiding reactions at first. After a few seconds he puckered up his face, began to nod his head and to look intently at the experimenter. He next began to push the rabbit away with his feet, withdrawing his body at the same time. Then as the rabbit came nearer he began pulling his feet away, nodding his head, and wailing "da da". After about a minute he reached out tentatively and slowly and touched the rabbit's ear with his right hand, finally manipulating it. The rabbit was again placed in his lap. Again he began to fret and withdrew his hands. He reached out tentatively with his left hand and touched the animal, shuddered and withdrew the whole body. The experimenter then took hold of his left hand and laid it on the rabbit's back. Albert immediately withdrew his hand and began to suck his thumb. Again the rabbit was laid in his lap. He began to cry, covering his face with both hands."

This... is a little disturbing...

PERSONAL NOTES

SUBJECT _Me and My Vivid Imagination_

YEAR _2014_

I sat listening to the news, unable to turn away. A flight had just gone down in the Ukraine, and the announcers were describing it in every grisly detail. I could feel my body tensing up and growing sluggish as my brain moved faster.

For an hour, I was with the newscaster, seeing every detail described on the phone call. My stomach lurched.

I knew I would be dealing with those fears again later, and I would have to choose whether or not to listen to them. I knew that if I wanted to deal with my fear, I should "capture" my thoughts and be aware of the thought patterns that I was creating.

I turned off the television; I had to for my own mental health. My vivid imagination was working against me.

There's good science behind this concept. When we imagine situations, our brains tend to produce a small echo of that emotion of the situation that we're imagining.[15] Almost as if it's actually occurring! So if we imagine something bad happening over and over, our brain is producing chemicals to make us more afraid.

. . . .

To be clear, I'm not talking about the process of mourning a loss or strategically thinking through a worst-case scenario. I mean constantly dwelling on every single bad thing that could happen and letting it play in your mind. I mean spending hours worrying and replaying events that you can't control.

My family would call this "getting yourself all worked up over nothing."

It's good to make a habit of picturing how well a situation could turn out. Focus on your dream coming true. After all, if you're going to imagine yourself trying something new and stepping out of your comfort zone, you might as well picture yourself rocking it.

Like a Hanson concert!

Our thoughts are powerful, and our imagination can strengthen or weaken our fear.

But our fear isn't just affected by our imagination. It's also affected by how we view fear itself.

It's a thought concept called *reframing*, and it completely changed how I dealt with fear.

```
┌────────────────────────────────────────────────┐
│                                                  │
│          P E R S O N A L   N O T E S             │
│                                                  │
│   SUBJECT Reframing: It's a Thinking Game        │
│   YEAR  Last Semester                            │
│                                                  │
└────────────────────────────────────────────────┘
```

I had always believed that fear was the sign of something horrible. That I had disobeyed some great commandment and was on a one-way track to a doomed existence of caffeine-free coffee and SEC football. I thought that once I stepped out to follow my dreams I would have absolutely no fear at all. And if I did have fear? Well, that meant that I was not on the right path—or certainly not gifted at whatever I was trying to do.

That was the way I viewed fear: that something was wrong and that I had already failed.

Nope. None of it was true.

But over and over, and every time I launched out to try something new, the fears hit me. And every time, I was surprised that I was afraid, as if this were a new emotion that I was completely unaware of.

Each time I felt fear, I freaked out and stopped everything. I questioned everything. I put everything on hold until I could figure out what was wrong or until I could overcome it. I bowed to its wishes and thanked it kindly for its lovely presence. Hung up its coat and served it tea and biscuits. Invited it to watch an episode of *Downton Abbey*.

....

It's true—I let fear completely shut me down and paralyze me. Until I realized that fear was merely a sign that I was out of my comfort zone. In fact, fear was actually a sign of a good thing. It meant I had an opportunity to become better.

FEAR IS JUST AN EMOTION.
IT IS NOT A SIGN.
IT IS NOT YOUR DESTINY.
It's just a temporary emotion. That's it.

That's one of the first steps in dealing with fear—to redefine what fear means in your thoughts. We call this *relabeling* or *reframing*. If you view fear differently, then it will affect you differently.

Author Jeff Wise explains it this way:

> One really powerful tool involves a kind of reframing: that is, teaching yourself to experience what you perceive as a negative stimulus—the churning gut, the racing heart, the sweaty palms—not as a negative thing, fear, but a positive one, excitement.[16]

Just changing the way you view fear changes the way it affects you. You may still feel it, but it no longer has the same importance in your mind. It makes the fear loop lessen instead of growing stronger.

While teaching a college class on marketing concepts recently, I saw firsthand with one of my students how powerful reframing can be.

....

I stood at the front of the class and waited for CJ* to step up to the projector screen. CJ did not look thrilled.

Me: Are you ready to give your presentation?

CJ: But, Kinda, I'm really . . . scared. I'm bad at this. My hands start shaking. I can't do it! I can't doooooo it! (Eyes grow wide. Starts to panic.)

Me: Hey, good! You should be scared. That's great.

CJ   Yes, I . . . wait, what?

Me: Yes, it's just fear. That means you care. And also, you won't fall asleep during the presentation now. Come on, it would be a little strange if you weren't afraid.

CJ: But you don't look scared.

Me: I'm not now. My stomach was in knots the entire first semester I taught. And I still get nervous every time I speak in a new place.

CJ: You do?

Me: Yeah, absolutely. It's part of it.

CJ: Oh. (Looks relieved). What do you do about it?

Me: First of all, when I'm scared, I stop and take a deep breath and feel the fear. I say, "Hey, look at that. Helloooo, fear. That's cool. Looks like I'm stepping out of my comfort zone. Thanks for helping pump enough blood to my brain to where I can think on my feet. I'm gonna kick some tail with this presentation."

CJ: But my hands shake.

Me: Eh, let them shake. It's part of it. It goes away.

CJ: It does? Nothing is wrong?

Me: Nothing is wrong. This is exactly where you're supposed to be in the process. Don't think of today as the day you have to be perfect. Think of it as you using the next ten presentations to get better and more relaxed. Go do your thing—it will work itself out. Go get 'em tiger! (I'm terrible at sounding cool.)

....

*Completely made-up name. Unless you're named CJ. Then this was totally about you.

This conversation inevitably happens every semester. The students are surprised and relieved to find out that they don't have to not be afraid. It's amazing how much their fear level will drop in a presentation or two just by them realizing that there's nothing wrong with being afraid. Once they know that the fear is okay, they're free to ignore it, and the body's alarm system starts quieting down. The death spiral weakens. It's funny how that works. It's reframing.

....

Reframe fear to where it doesn't have as much power:

You can say it's positive.
You can say it's silly.
You can say it's something there to help you.
You can say it's not you—it's just your fear.
You can say it's a child throwing a temper tantrum who is learning to behave.
You can say it's a growth sign that you're stepping outside of your comfort zone.

Whatever works for you—relabel fear to be something you welcome as getting one step closer to what you want to accomplish.

Just changing that thought weakens the power that fear has over you. I recently experienced the power of reframing in a different way . . . the most embarrassing way possible. In skinny jeans. On a stage. With everything going horribly wrong.

....

Fear shows up when you:

- Follow a dream.
- Choose to leave an unhealthy relationship (significant other, friend, family member).
- Branch out and meet new friends.
- Travel to a new place.
- Try just about anything new.

Things they don't tell you:

- You'll have knots in the pit of your stomach when you step out to do something you're supposed to do.
- You might be terrified for a while.
- You may really suck at first, and you'll probably make mistakes.
- Things will never go as smoothly as planned.

Top signs you're getting ready to do something out of your comfort zone:

- A seven-year-old kid just told you to calm down and offered you a brown paper bag.
- The waitress just gave you a coffee and said, "It's on the house, you look terrible."
- You considered faking a contagious disease to avoid it.
- You actually prayed for a contagious disease to avoid it.
- You've been on social media for seven hours to avoid thinking about it.

....

```
┌─────────────────────────────────────────┐
│  ┌───────────────────────────────────┐  │
│  │                                   │  │
│  │        PERSONAL NOTES             │  │
│  │                                   │  │
│  │  SUBJECT  Reframing: The Red Pants │  │
│  │  YEAR  Present Day                 │  │
│  │                                   │  │
│  └───────────────────────────────────┘  │
└─────────────────────────────────────────┘
```

"Pssssst . . . hey, Kinda! Hey!" The girl waved her hand up at me tentatively from her seat in the front row, then she put it back down. The friend next to her fidgeted back and forth in her chair and stared at me wide-eyed, her eyes sending me unspoken messages. A third girl shook her head anxiously and pointed to the original hand-waver. "Hey, Kinda . . . Hey!"

I pulled my barstool up to the middle of the stage and leaned up against it, relief relaxing my mouth into a smile. I had made it through another round of speaking on a stage, and now it was time for the Q&A. Unscripted. No deep wisdom to impart. Just fun randomness. I motioned to the girls waving at me from the front row and spoke into the mike, "I think someone here was first. You're next!"

They nodded politely. They looked worried.

"Hey, girls! Whatcha got for me?"

In unison, they all leaned forward. Unconsciously, I leaned in too. They motioned me closer. I pulled the mike down away from our voices.

. . . .

"Hey, we think you might have something . . . there." One girl spoke. Another gestured toward me . . . toward my backside. "Did you sit in something? On a piece of tape?"

And instinctively I knew. There was nothing on me. I smiled at the girls and slowly backed toward the barstool in the middle of the stage.

My red skinny jeans had ripped up the back. Onstage. In the middle of speaking. Some time after the opening dance and before me doing a sarcastic "drop it" move on the stage.

Cue William Shatner voice: My pants. Had. Ripped. Onstage. Facepalm.

. . . .

You think when you start a project, *What's the worst that can happen?* And I had thought of quite a few options about public speaking. I could trip and fall behind the podium. I could slip up and say a curse word into the mike. I could have an epic tumble off the front of the stage.

I thought of those things, you know. They went through my mind every time before I walked onstage.

Every. Time.

And now, standing on the stage, staring back at the glare from the spotlights, and knowing that part of my jeans were missing at the rear, it made me want to laugh.

. . . .

This wasn't so bad. Nothing tragic had happened. No one had leaked the story to the *National Enquirer*. No one cared.

No, it wasn't so bad after all.

I felt a bit more freedom than I had the day before. (And not because my jeans weren't as tight anymore.)

That's the funny thing about fear—many of the things we fear aren't as bad as we give them credit for. In fact, we spend more time in terror of possibilities than anything else. Most things, if they actually happened, wouldn't be so bad.

The anticipation of the event is more frightening than the event itself. It's that imagination we talked about earlier that creates the panic.

Chip and Dan Heath have an interesting perspective on this decision-making process in their book *Decisive*. They ask if we make a decision, what will we say:

> Five minutes from now
> Five months from now
> Five years from now[17]

It takes away the temporary crazies of our emotions and asks what is really important. I like to apply that concept to fear as well. If the things that you're afraid of actually do happen, what will your emotions be in the future? I applied that to my red pants situation.

Five minutes from now: I would be a little embarrassed.

Five months from now: I would be telling the story and giggling about it.

Five years from now: I would be hiding the fact that I ever wore red skinny jeans anywhere.

None of those things would be worth not speaking in public for. In fact, I don't think any of those things were worth worrying about. They weren't even worth taking up a space in my mind. Yes, something could go wrong if I stepped out and followed my heart, but was it worth lying in bed at night worrying with knots in my stomach?

No. The answer was no.

It didn't mean that I wouldn't still worry or be fearful on occasion, of course. It just meant that I wouldn't give a valid place to that in my life. I wouldn't focus on it, because it wouldn't help anything.

And again, like with the earlier reframing, it helped to make the fear less important in my mind, and I walked a little further from the Swirling Vortex of Doom.

Our thoughts are powerful. By choosing to focus on our dreams instead of fear, our fear weakens. By simply shrugging our shoulders to the fear and not getting upset that it is there, the fear loses power. Our thoughts help us walk away from the Swirling Vortex of Doom.

And, as it turns out, so do the behaviors that we choose. Enter Dr. Schwartz and little heaters.

. . . .

RESEARCH NOTES

SUBJECT Dr. Schwartz

YEAR 1992

Dr. Jeffrey Schwartz spent decades studying the human brain, and his specialty was obsessive compulsive disorders (OCD). For years he listened to people's stories of how OCD had crippled their lives, essentially hijacking their ability to get through the day. They would get stuck in repetitive echoing loops of thoughts and behaviors, and it was paralyzing to them.

Dr. Schwartz knew that there was more going on than met the eye, so he devised a plan. He used PET (positron emission tomography) to analyze what happened when people faced uncomfortable situations. When studying OCD, he found something interesting. When people faced phobias or things that made them terribly afraid, the orbital cortex in their brain actually overheated and the people felt paralyzed to move forward.[18] It *overheated*.

Yep.

That was me.

My brain was a little heater.

. . . .

Every time I faced something new or made an important decision, it felt as if my brain were heating up. I felt paralyzed.

You don't have to have OCD to know what it feels like to have your brain overheat. To get stuck in the middle of a stressful decision and to have your brain just shut down. To step out to do something new, feel afraid, and just panic. Or to have worries and fears just crowd your mind until there's no room left for anything else.

Dr. Schwartz kept researching this overheating orbital cortex phenomenon and saw a glimmer of hope spelled out in the bold red and yellow colors of the PET scan. He found that when people focused on behavior therapy—on moving forward—they could actually change the chemical reactions in their brains. Scans showed that their brains began processing fears differently and the caudate nucleus, deep in the brain, cooled down. It no longer overheated.[19] Those who wanted to reach a goal but also had paralyzing fear had to temporarily ignore their emotions and go forward to something better.

They used cognitive behavior therapy. They had fear and anxiety, but they went against their emotions and chose their behavior. They focused on what was important. They chose what was right, even though it felt uncomfortable.

Says Schwartz: "It's not how you feel, it's what you do that counts. Because when you do the right things, feelings tend to improve as a matter of course."[20] He also makes the point, "If I change my behavior, I'll actually be changing the way my brain works."[21]

....

That meant that they didn't focus on how afraid they were. They didn't even try not to be afraid, as I mentioned with the earlier reframing. They switched their focus and attention to just doing the behavior that they knew was healthy. They walked in the direction they knew they should be going, even if they felt terribly uncomfortable.

They chose the behavior they knew was right until their emotions lined up with it.

What did that mean for me? Well, it meant that the only way to go forward with my dream was to recognize my fear but keep going. If I knew deep within my heart of hearts that I needed to do something, I needed to push past the fear that I felt. The calmer emotions would probably come later.

I hoped.

I had a chance to test out this behavioral strategy a short time later . . . while I was dangling from a cable high in the mountains and trembling like a nervous chihuahua.

> When your emotions are frantic—
> Choose the behavior. Choose what
> you know is true. The feelings will
> come later.

....

PERSONAL NOTES

SUBJECT _Me vs. the Mountain_

YEAR _2012_

I had talked about the mountaintop restaurant for months; I was giddy about the possibility. I had blabbed about it to every available friend or stranger and pictured it in my mind for weeks. It would be life-changing. I would glide up the mountain while doing a small tap dance in the cable car. Onlookers would be so impressed with my sense of adventure and rhythm that they would write home to their loved ones about it on vintage, artificially faded hipster postcards. It would be amazing.

And then I got there and actually saw the cable cars—taking people straight up the side of the mountain.

Straight.
Up.
The.
Side.

I'm from Oklahoma originally, and we don't have real mountains there. We have the world's largest hill—just a foot shy of being an actual mountain—but that doesn't count. These were _mountains_.

....

I stood there, staring at the honest-to-goodness mountains with the clear boxes dangling on cables in the air above them. It made my stomach queasy, but I knew I was trapped. If I didn't do it, I would regret it, and everyone else would know I had chickened out. Man, was I wishing I had kept my big mouth shut.

I bought the ticket and stepped onto the cable car.

The cables started whirring and the cable car went over the first support pole—and started swaying back and forth. I looked down and started leaning over. I did my usual frantic "why-am-I-up-in-the-air-what's-going-on" look around. The Australian young lady next to me asked, "Are you going to be okay?" I nodded yes and leaned over in a hunched position toward the middle of the car so I couldn't see outside.

Everyone thought I was about to throw up. Never have I ever seen an area clear so fast in my life. They made a nice clear area around me, and I had my nice little American personal space back. So I learned something. If people aren't giving you your personal space—lean over, twenty-degree angle forward, clutch your stomach, and look very worried. My friend stood at the side of the cable car, chuckling at the people-free halo around me.

Somewhere about halfway up the mountain on the cable car with me nervously clinging to the pole, I remember hearing this inside me: *Why don't you just enjoy this? You might as well. You'll have to ride it, and you'll get to the top either way. Why don't you just act as if everything is fine, because it probably will be.*

....

I'll say it was God, because I like to think God still has time to ride up cable cars and get sarcastic with me when I'm terrified.

The conversation in my head went something like this:

God: Why don't you just enjoy this?

Me: I don't know if you realize this, God, but I'm helping the cable car here. My fear and worry are actually keeping it in the air. You obviously don't realize this.

God: Well, why don't you pretend? Then if it doesn't crash, at least you will have enjoyed the ride.

Everything inside me went strangely calm, and I thought about it. It was true. Either I was about to die on the side of the most beautiful mountain in the world in one of the most freakish accidents in the history of the country, or I would make it to the top. Either way, I was missing the view. My clinging to the pole and staring at the floor wasn't holding the cable car together.

....

And so I decided to pretend as if I weren't afraid.

I slowly pulled myself to the edge of the car and looked out the window. I stood up straight and stretched out my fingers and started taking deeper breaths. By this time, we were getting high into the mountains and clouds were nearing. I nervously pulled out my camera and started filming. The view was beautiful.

My heart pounded like I was James Bond filming the movie that the restaurant had become so famous for, and then it gradually slowed to a more-normal rhythm. I was quite sure this process mimicked the fear-inducing *Bachelor* show dates, and had any single men been around, we would have instantly fallen in love.

The car ascended into the clouds, and a hush fell over everyone around me. We were a floating glass car in the middle of clouds. Visions of *Charlie and the Great Glass Elevator* flashed through my mind. All we could see was white.

A few seconds later, the clouds broke and we could see the car whizzing by the steep rocky cliffs, mere feet from us. I sucked my breath in. Up we went through the last of the clouds. The car tipped and swayed to a slow stop. There it was: the restaurant on the top of the mountain.

We had arrived.

....

I've looked back at that experience several times and wondered why my

....

emotions could calm when the obvious danger was still present. I knew my thoughts could affect my emotions. I found out that my physical behaviors could as well.

Think about this example:

When we are happy, we tend to smile. When we are sad, we slump down and carry our entire body in a downcast manner. When we are fearful, our bodies tense up and our heart rate increases.

But the opposite is also true. If you stand up straight and smile, you tend to become happier. And if you tense your body up and adopt a posture of being nervous, you tend to become more nervous.

Your physical behaviors affect your emotions.

John Riskind and Carolyn Gotay conducted an experiment to see how much postures affected people's emotions. They had some people stand in a confident manner—upright and expansive. They had another group stand in a manner that would be sad or depressed—slumped down. They found that the subjects who stood in a confident manner tended to feel more confident and experience less stress.[22]

In another experiment, Sandra Duclos and her team put subjects into three groups and had each stand in a manner that would indicate 1) fearfulness 2) sadness 3) anger. They found that the subjects' feelings "came to match precisely those associated with the postures they had adopted."[23] For instance, those who were asked to sit in a fearful posture became more fearful.

. . . .

What does all of this mean? It means that we have two ways that we can deal with fear. One way is to intentionally choose healthy, life-giving thoughts. The other way is to choose healthy behaviors even when we do not have happy emotions.

We can take steps to calm our bodies when our minds are racing.

We can stand tall when we feel otherwise and take breaths deeper than our valor. We can walk as if we owned the world even while we are still filling out a loan application for it.

We can look life in the eye like the people of strength that we are and will someday be. We can choose the behavior that will take us one more step away from the Swirling Vortex of Doom.

Yes, we do have power, and we have choices. Even the small choices make a difference to make our fear stronger or weaker.

Which brings me to tornadoes.

I Made it!

PERSONAL NOTES

SUBJECT _The Hook Echo_

YEAR _1953_

It was a dark and stormy night on Thursday, April 9, 1953. No, really—
it was.[24]

Don Staggs and his assistant traveled to the radar station at the Willard
Airport in Champaign, Illinois. A piece had broken on the radar scope,
and Don was just the guy to fix it. He was a radar technician with the
Illinois State Water Survey Staff. Don replaced the piece on the radar
and went about the process of testing it.

And thus began a beautiful chain of coincidences that allowed a crucial
discovery to be made.

Had Don not decided to test the radar at that very time, the radar
wouldn't have been left on. It was early evening, and the radar was
usually off during that time period.

Meanwhile, a strong tornado began to occur north of one of the few
radars in the country equipped for weather research. And because the
storm was north of the radar station, there was no rain interference on
the radar.

....

Don didn't know any of this at the time.

As Don began going through the repair tests, he noticed a strange circular pattern forming on the radar scope. The reading wasn't quite like anything he had seen recorded before. He turned on the 35mm camera attached to the radar scope—also one of the few in the country, another coincidence—and began filming.

Don Staggs would realize later that he had filmed the first tornado hook echo ever recorded on radar.

This discovery of a hook echo—or "tornado echo," as they called it in their 1954 survey report—meant that there were certain indicators that allowed meteorologists to predict where a tornado might occur.

One of these indicators was the distinct pattern of a circular hook-like vortex on the radar screen. It meant all of the characteristics were there to form a tornado and that danger was present.

It was a game changer. Tracking and predicting tornadoes with radars was in its infancy. Meteorologists weren't even sure what patterns indicated that a tornado was forming.

This weather pattern recording helped blaze a trail to form the first US national weather radar network.

The hook echo.

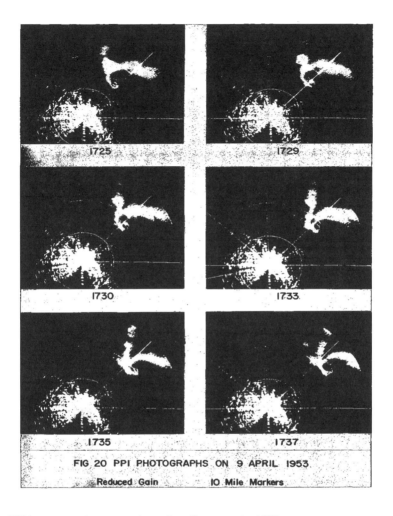

FIG 20 PPI PHOTOGRAPHS ON 9 APRIL 1953.
Reduced Gain   10 Mile Markers

We've come a long way since that discovery in 1953.

Now every person in the Midwest grows up knowing about Doppler radars and weather patterns. Tornado season comes around every year like football season, and a strange foreboding excitement charges the air

....

when the sky darkens and the leaves flip over. We read the radar screens with the ease of a paint-by-number coloring book, and meteorologists become local legends with their stormcasting. *When they take off their jacket, it's serious!* And you're not truly from the Midwest if you can't look at a radar screen and find the hook echo.

The hook echo is easy to spot; it looks like the outline of a hook on the radar. It shows the wind circulating in such a way that it's right at the edge of danger—it's a warning, if you will.

It's just at that point when the characteristics are there for a tornado. The storm will go one of two ways: it will either dissipate harmlessly or suddenly pick up and start swirling into a potentially dangerous tornado.

....

I looked at the hook echoes on the radar screen printouts and couldn't help but think that it looked suspiciously like a Swirling Vortex of Doom. It all sounded much too familiar.

That hook echo was the crucial time in the storm formation. Everything was there for it to strengthen or weaken. It was a lot like what I was dealing with in my Swirling Vortex of Doom.

I had those moments of awareness when I felt myself going into fear and anxiety, and I knew it was going to take me aside into a deadly swirling concoction of distraction and fear.

....

STATE OF ILLINOIS
William G. Stratton, Governor

STUDY OF AN ILLINOIS TORNADO USING RADAR, SYNOPTIC WEATHER AND FIELD SURVEY DATA

BY

F. A. HUFF, H. W. HISER and S. G. BIGLER

Department of Registration and Education
Vera M. Binks, Director

STATE WATER SURVEY DIVISION
A. M. BUSWELL, Chief
Urbana, Illinois

TABLE OF CONTENTS

Page

INTRODUCTION

Since the advent of radar as a meteorological research and forecasting tool during World War II, there has been considerable speculation among radar meteorologists as to whether or not it would be possible for radar to detect a tornado. Due to the limited size of tornadoes which average about 250 yards in diameter[1], it has sometimes been postulated that such violent storms would occur undetected by radar, especially at long range. Even at short range it has been thought that thunderstorm activity might mask the tornadic activity, or that insufficient reflectivity from the tornado might limit the utility of radar for detection purposes. Observers of radar scopes have reported, however, that unusually large and strong echoes are present when tornado conditions develop,.

During the afternoon of 9 April 1953, the Water Survey was operating its AN/APS-15A (3-cm) radar for the routine collection of rainfall data in conjunction with a research project to determine the utility of radar for the quantitative measurement of precipitation. During the late afternoon, the development, growth, and movement of a tornado echo associated with a thunderstorm echo was observed on the radar scope and photographed in detail. This distinct tornado echo, which was observed near the southwest edge of the associated thunderstorm, contained the tornado funnel which reached the surface and caused about four million dollars damage in east-central Illinois . The actual position of the surface funnel was not visible within the tornado echo on the plan-position indicator (PPI). Although the radar operator, who incidentally was not a meteorologist, recognized the unusual nature of the PPI echo and the possibility of a tornado,, positive identification was not made at the time of the radar tracking.

To the best of the authors' knowledge, this was the first time that such a tornado echo had been observed and photographed in detail, although an interesting radar observation during a tornado situation was reported by the Air Weather Service in 1945[11]. Their set at Maxwell Field, Alabama was on the air at the time a tornado was reported in the area. A precipitation area shaped like a "6" was detected and this shape was maintained during the tornado activity. Unfortunately, radar scope photographs of the storm were not made.

Since the Illinois tornado, there have been other radar observations and photographs made of tornado echoes by several other radar research groups. Consequently, it may be concluded that radar is capable of detecting tornado situations under favorable conditions, and that meteorologists have a new tool for the investigation of the causes of tornado formation. Furthermore, the possibility exists that as more radar tornado data are collected and research progresses, it may be possible to establish radar storm warning systems in tornado areas to reduce loss of lives, and to some extent, property damage.

The purpose of this report is: (1) to present detailed data on the 9 April 1953 tornado for information and use in tornado research; and (2) to make data relevant to the appearance of tornado echoes on the radar scope available to meteorologists, in the hope that it will aid and stimulate interest in radar observational programs to gather more tornado data. Included in the report are: a summary of synoptic conditions with illustrative weather charts; a large number of radar photos showing development and movement of the tornado echo, with a discussion of interesting features; and, the results of a detailed field survey along the tornado path in Illinois for correlation with the synoptic weather data and radar data.

Discussion of Existing Criteria For Tornado Formation

Fawbush, Miller, and Starrett have devised a method for forecasting tornadoes based upon the existence of certain synoptic conditions a few hours prior to tornado formation[6]. Briefly summarized, the synoptic conditions which must be fulfilled are:

1. A layer of moist air near the surface must be surmounted by a deep layer of dry air.

2. A distinct moisture wedge or ridge must be present in the moist layer.

3. The winds aloft must exhibit a maximum of speed along a relatively narrow band at some level between 10,000 feet and 20,000 feet, with the maximum speed exceeding 35 knots.

4. The vertical projection of the axis of wind maximum must intersect the moisture ridge axis.

5. The temperature distribution of the air column as a whole must indicate conditional instability.

6. The moist layer must be subjected to considerable lifting.

Note to self: I have too many "favorable criteria" for a death spiral. Must change that...

Fawbush and Miller amplified these forecasting criteria with the presentation of a mean tornado sounding in 1952, which was mentioned earlier. Reference to the various surface and upper air charts and the Rantoul radiosonde for 1500 CST indicates that the Fawbush and Miller criteria were generally satisfied in east-central Illinois at the time of the tornado formation.

Tepper has indicated that the intersection of two pressure jump lines is a preferred location for tornado development[10]. Except for those shown in figure 5, barograph records for Illinois and Indiana stations were not available for a pressure jump analysis. As previously mentioned, pressure jumps were not reported by Illinois stations on hourly sequences during the afternoon, although there were several jumps reported in Indiana in conjunction with the evening squall zone.

Showalter has presented both a thunderstorm stability index and a tornado index, both of which may be used to indicate the probability of tornadoes[8]. These indices are based upon thermodynamic considerations, the details of which will not be repeated here. Showalter states that a zero or negative tornado index indicates probable tornadoes when associated with a zero or negative thunderstorm stability index. He points out that experience to date indicates a very high probability of tornadoes in any warm sector that shows negative values of -4 or greater on both the stability index and the tornado index. The Rantoul radiosonde for 1500 CST indicated a -1 for the tornado index and -5 for the thunderstorm stability index. The thunderstorm stability index for Columbia at 0900 CST was +1, while the tornado index was +2. Columbia was the nearest station to the central Illinois area which was in the warm air mass at that time.

The Tornado Echo

At 1653 CST (figure 13), a small, weak echo appeared at the southwest edge of the thunderstorm echo. About 1658 CST (figure 13), an appendage appeared on the northwest edge of the thunderstorm echo; however, this appendage dissipated about 10 minutes later. By 1700 CST (figure 13), the echo at the southwest edge of the thunderstorm had developed and expanded southward. The surface tornado developed a few minutes later from this echo, which will henceforth be referred to as the tornado echo. The tornado echo extended three to four miles beyond the edge of the thunderstorm echo. A flat "V" began forming on the north side of the associated thunderstorm echo about this time. This was probably due to attenuation. At 1705 CST (figure 14), Rantoul (RAN) was on the edge of this "V", and a surface observation taken at that time indicated a heavy thunderstorm and heavy hail in progress. Reduced gain observations indicated that the heaviest precipitation was occurring a few miles south of Rantoul. An apparent appendage can be seen on the cloud at the north edge of the scope at this time (figure 14). However, no tornadoes were reported with this cloud at this time or later, although heavy hail did occur with it. Note the sharply defined edge of the thunderstorm echo near the tornado echo, indicating the presence of a strong moisture gradient. Reference to the reduced gain photographs in figure 19 shows a separation between the tornado echo and the thunderstorm echo in the early stages of the tornado development, indicating the presence of a separate core or cell in the tornado circulation.

The tornado echo continued to develop, and about 1713 CST (figure 14), the tornado reached the surface west of Leverett at a point approximately ten miles north of the radar station. At this time, the tornado's surface position was at the southern end of the tornado echo appearing on the PPI. At the time of the first surface damage, the tornado echo was about four miles long and just beginning to develop cyclonic curl. This curl developed at a rate of about 60 knots.

The tornado echo was plainly visible for at least 10 minutes before the tornado reached the ground. Six to seven steps (gain reductions) were required to extinguish the tornado echo during this time, indicating the presence of appreciable water, either in the liquid or solid state. These steps are 22 and 28 decibels below the maximum receiver sensitivity of 97 decibels (Table II).

It is of interest at this time to summarize the observation of Major Carl D. Mitchell, a Chanute Air Force Base Weather Officer, who observed the formation of this tornado from his home on the north side of Urbana, about three miles south of the surface path. Prior to the formation of the tornado, he observed five or six projections, apparently tornado funnels, from the bottom of the thunderstorm cloud. He estimated that they each lasted for about 15 seconds and dissipated. They appeared to extend only a few hundred feet below the cloud base and were much paler than the thunderstorm cloud. When the tornado formed, it appeared to reach the ground in the form of a column rather than a funnel. It appeared to be a vertical column with oscillation of the base near the ground. Major Mitchell indicated that the thunderstorm cloud was the only cloud with strong development in the area just prior to the tornado formation.

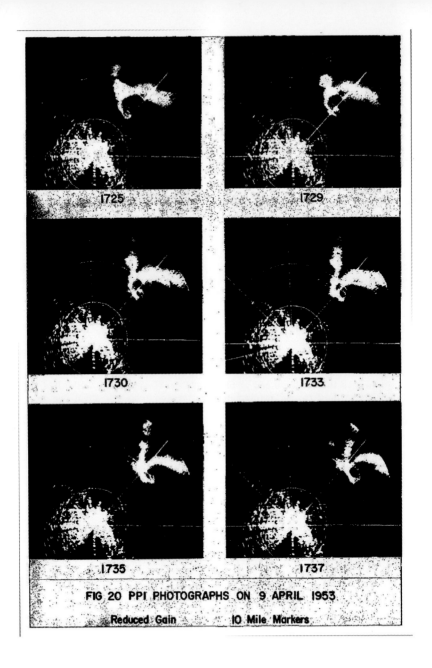

1725   1729

1730   1733

1735   1737

FIG 20 PPI PHOTOGRAPHS ON 9 APRIL 1953

Reduced Gain   10 Mile Markers

FIG. 28 TORNADO AS OBSERVED FROM POSITION "A" BETWEEN 1715 AND 1720 CST LOOKING SOUTH

a. Funnel Approximately 7 Miles Away

b. Funnel Approximately $2\frac{1}{2}$ Miles Away

c. Funnel Approximately 2 Miles Away

FIG. 29 TORNADO AS OBSERVED FROM POSITION "B" BETWEEN 1745 AND 1800 C.S.T. LOOKING WEST-NORTHWEST

CONCLUSIONS

1. Radar is capable of detecting and tracking tornado-producing echoes under favorable conditions, thus providing a valuable tool for tornado research.

2. The appearance of an appendage on a precipitation echo is not a rare occurrence and does not necessarily denote the presence of a tornado. For example, appendages were observed on several echoes outside of the tornado area on 9 April. Also, there is insufficient evidence at present to conclude that tornadoes occur only in conjunction with an appendage or a parasite echo (tornado echo) along the associated precipitation echo. Observations and photographs appearing in the literature indicate that tornadoes may also originate from within the associated cloud. Furthermore, when a tornado echo is present, attenuation due to range and intervening precipitation may appreciably reduce the effective detection range of the tornado echo. This is especially true with 3-cm radar where precipitation attenuation may be significant.

3. However, the Illinois observations and others made later in 1953 show that well-defined tornado echoes do sometimes occur. The continued growth of a parasite echo or appendage with development of cyclonic curl and/or an "eye", such as in the Illinois tornado, may be a positive indication of a tornado. However, more data are needed before the utility and limitations of radar in tornado detection can be defined. Possibly large tornadoes, such as the tornado cyclone mentioned by Brooks , are typified by the Illinois tornado while small tornadoes originate from within the associated thunderstorm cloud. (Large here refers to tornado size and not necessarily the associated property damage).

Walk away...

4. Although radar is capable of detecting a tornado-producing echo and its associated thunderstorm echo, the present data do not indicate that the exact position of the surface tornado funnel can be visually observed within the tornado echo mass on the radar scope. The radar integrates the echo mass within the volume of its beam, and in the case of the 9 April tornado, the areal extent of the surface funnel was much less than that of the tornado-producing echo, although the size of the surface funnel was considerably greater than the average for tornadoes. However, as more data are collected, some means of positioning the surface funnel within the echo mass may be revealed.

5. The use of radar having both plan-position indicators and range-height indicators is desirable for the collection of tornado research data, so that a three-dimensional picture of the storms can be obtained.

Study of an Illinois Tornado Using Radar, Synoptic Weather and Field Survey Data (1954), by F.A. Huff, H.W. Hiser, and S.G. Bigler, Report of Investigation 22, Illinois State Water Survey.

If I let it. If I walked in that direction and let my mind take me there. I knew it would take me into a death spiral if I worked myself up over it and focused on fear instead of faith.

We all have those hook echo moments when we feel fear and anxiety starting to build. We know if we concentrate on that anxious thought or choose that unhealthy behavior, it will lead us further into the vortex. Half of our afternoon will be lost because of anxious thoughts, and we'll have nothing to show for it but knots in our stomach.

At those times, we can make choices to let the Swirling Vortex pick up speed or make choices so that it will weaken and dissipate.

It's a process, and it takes time, but we can do it.

I paged through the old pictures of that first hook echo. I was determined to start walking away from my death spiral. It was time to gather everything I had learned and start walking it out. And I was hoping if I did, I could unlearn a bit of fear. And learn a bit of freedom.

....

BEHAVIORS

- Stand tall, put your hands on your hips, and take deep breaths.
- Practice deep breathing and relaxation techniques. I like to count to ten breathing in and out. It switches my focus from the fear to calming down.
- Have a game plan ahead of time for how you will respond to the fear—that way you'll feel more in control. I have silly television shows on my laptop and gossip magazines (gasp!) that I bring to read on a plane when we hit turbulence. I'm prepared for dealing with it. Bam! Take that, fear.
- Start small to gain confidence. If you want to speak to stadiums, start by speaking at whatever small groups you can.

THOUGHTS

- Reframing: Redefine fear as being something that is welcome and is taking you out of your comfort zone.
- Keep things in perspective. Most things we fear aren't really that fearful in themselves.
- Watch your imagination: That movie that's playing in your head? Have it focus on the dream instead of the fear.
- Have a support system to encourage and empower you.

. . . .

PERSONAL NOTES

SUBJECT *The Fear You SHOULD Listen To*

YEAR *Present Day*

I should make a note here that there are two kinds of fears in the world: the kind you should listen to, and the kind you shouldn't.

One kind is gut instinct, the instinctual feeling from the depth of your soul that something is wrong, is off. The "knowing" deep within you that something or someone cannot be trusted. The feeling that you should leave a situation.

That's the kind to listen to.

I've always had a tough time with this, particularly because I've dealt with obsessive phobia fears that scream at you to panic in random and harmless situations. They jump out from behind innocent corners with terrifying gremlin masks and taunt you not to be afraid.

And so whenever I have been fearful, my quandary has always been this: Is this fear legit, or just me? Is this worth worrying about, or is it my brain playing tricks on me?

And this is what I have learned.

....

Your instinct—that voice deep in your spiritual being—is calm and assured and directive. That's the fear that you should listen to: your gut instinct deep inside that tells you something is wrong.

There's another voice of fear that is panicked and repetitive. It's not helpful or directive; it's simply anxious. Listen a little deeper than that to your instinct instead of the panic.

At the core of our beings, each one of us knows the difference. We know when we are supposed to pursue a dream and ignore the voice of fear. And we know in our gut when something is wrong.

That repetitive and panicked voice of worry and fear? That's what we need to walk away from. That's the Swirling Vortex of Doom. That's the death spiral.

....

```
┌─────────────────────────────────────────────────────┐
│                                                       │
│           PERSONAL NOTES                              │
│                                                       │
│   SUBJECT  Where Am I Now?                            │
│                                                       │
│   YEAR  Present Day                                   │
│                                                       │
└─────────────────────────────────────────────────────┘
```

This unlearning fear thing—it's a process, not a step.

You have to give yourself room to grow and make mistakes, and you have to realize that you might be uncomfortable for a while.

You can unlearn fears and learn freedom from the death circle, but that takes being willing to step out of your comfort zone. And it takes being out of your comfort zone long enough in a healthy way to where your brain finally calms down and realizes it's not in crisis mode anymore. It sometimes helps to slowly step out and conquer the fear in small pieces if you can. It just takes a bit of time. It's a process, not a step.

I am a process

Every time I step out of my comfort zone, I still get the echoing loop of fear and anxiety in my brain. It grows stronger the closer I get to a stage, and it screams the minutes before I walk in front of a mike. It loops and echoes, and I feel my orbital cortex heating up. And I shake my head. And I sigh. I realize it's a hook echo signaling a swirling vortex on the horizon.

And I walk in front of the crowd and start talking, because if I stop to listen to the echoing loop in my head—if I ask fear's permission—it will never tell me go. The fear will *never* tell me to go.

....

The fear will never say, "You know what? I think I'm going to give her a break today. I think I'll let her go through this one easily. She won't worry at all, and she'll sleep peacefully every night." If I ask the fear, it will never say that. It will never give me rest, and I will get stuck in paralysis.

And so I focus on what really matters. I remember the death spiral, and I decide to leave the circle. I switch my focus, I start to walk in a different direction, and I do it scared.

And that's how we stop fear's death spiral. We recognize the hook echo signal. We realize that fear is just an emotion. We switch our focus. We look toward our goal, and we take healthy steps. Fear loses power when we find more important things to focus on. We take a deep breath. And we walk on. We do it scared.

You have that power to decide that fear should stop making decisions for your life. Even when it's uncomfortable, you can start to listen to fear a little less today than you did yesterday.

You can start taking action and going in the right direction in the middle of the fear.

You can still walk toward your dreams while you're sweating bullets.
You can have faith while you're terrified.
You can focus on something greater than the fear.
You were not meant to live afraid. You can break out of the death spiral.

This year I have learned that there is more of a peace in the failing than the fear of it. Given the chance, I'd Jump again

---

PERSONAL NOTES

SUBJECT *Kinda Landing (in) the Plane*

YEAR *Later in 2011*

I'm not up in the air; I'm just on a bus. I'm not up in the air; I'm just on a bus. This is a pothole; I'm just on a bus.

The plane bumped and sunk a bit lower. I could see the rows of houses coming into view below me through the misty clouds.

I took a breath and tried to stop my legs from shaking. That whole fight or flight thing was a real pain in the neck if I couldn't run or didn't have things that needed kicking.

Two weeks later and my legs had stopped shaking from fright and were shaking from the unexpected exercise of trekking across Italy and Switzerland. My travel buddy booked her ticket back home to the states. I stayed.

I had been scared for so long—scared of everything. Scared of being me. Scared of saying something stupid. Scared of messing up. Scared of change. Scared of dying. I was tired of being scared, and something in me just switched.

....

I decided to stay. Not even in spite of the fact that I was scared. I decided to stay *because* I was scared.

So it was there on the border of Switzerland and Germany that I arranged to have an epic fear showdown. I'm pretty sure it went against everything wise that I was supposed to do about conquering fears in small, incremental pieces.

But I waved good-bye to my friend, put on my backpack, and jumped on a train.

I wish I could have filmed that moment. It was so heroic. For about five minutes. Then I lost my balance and ended up stuck upside down with my pack strapped on—with people pointing and giggling at me. I was essentially a giant American turtle flipped upside down on a Swiss train. That was Thursday.

On Friday, I got trapped in a hailstorm and thought Oklahoma tornadoes were coming. I was the only person in Germany, I'm sure, to be ducking and covering in a doorway. And I was scared. And I cried.

On Saturday, I sat on the wrong half of a train and ended up in the middle of nowhere in Germany instead of back in Switzerland. And I sat in the train station alone. And I was scared. And I cried.

I came home three days earlier than I was supposed to. I switched my ticket in panicked anxiety at a free-WiFi Starbucks in Zurich. Failure? Maybe. I wasn't quite prepared.

....

But I stayed five days longer than my comfort zone wanted me to. And I made some of the most amazing memories I've ever had in my life.

And every time I traveled and flew after that, I became less scared. Eventually the other passengers on planes didn't offer me free drinks or random medications, and the toddlers stopped looking at me with annoyance.

That was progress. It was a process.

Two years later, I did the unthinkable and started a travel company with one of my best friends.

Me—the girl who had been terrified of flying. Me—the girl who had looked longingly at everyone else flying overseas and thought she could never go.

That girl voluntarily agreed to put herself on a plane and help other people overcome their fears and travel overseas. That girl was writing online tutorials on how to deal with anxiety while traveling.

I look back at how far I've come, and it's a little surreal. Not because I never get scared, because I do. But because somehow through all of that initial fear, I had kept walking. And it makes me proud. Proud of myself for focusing on my dream and going forward scared.

Proud of myself for stretching a little further toward peace and freedom and walking a little further away from the Swirling Vortex of Doom.

....

And if I can do it, anyone can. The flight attendants from that first Italy flight will back me up on that.

We aren't helpless. The death spiral doesn't have to win. We can keep walking through fear.

We can walk away from the death spiral, and just like the little army ants that William Beebe observed, we can do some serious damage after all.

May 23, 2011
I got up this morning and it was a bit like a load had lifted. I can breathe more easily now. The slight panic comes and goes, but I'm doing better. I got on a train to Füssen, and I realized that for a time, I wasn't afraid. And it's odd to say, but I actually teared up on the train. I'm sure passengers were wondering about the crazy American. But I was just picturing my life free from fear and the hope that it could actually be a possibility. What freedom. What a wondrous life that would be. Thoughts still come, but I'm trying to live in the moment.

....

PART IV

RESONATING FREEDOM

....

ECHO [EK-OH]

...

7. (noun)
A close parallel or repetition of an
idea, feeling, style, or event.

...

"His love for her found an echo in her own feelings."

RESEARCH NOTES

SUBJECT The Matter in the Mess

YEAR Very Recently

The bad part about writing is that you can't choose when the words come to you. Not the good ones.

I sat in front of my smudged and dusty laptop screen and willed the words to come. Nothing. My phone buzzed and begged me with notifications, and I halfheartedly typed a paragraph to spite it.

I knew what was slowing me down. It had been circling about in my head for a while now—that question I wasn't supposed to think or say. It had stayed my momentum at every turn and forced a hesitation to my step.

I looked at the dismal paragraph on the screen, and I felt myself wondering again.

Does all of this really matter? Do all of these hours—any of these words—do they really make a difference? Do I make a difference?

I knew what I was *supposed* to say in answer to that. I knew the technical jargon and quotes pulled from calendars too inspirational to feel

....

comfortable on my semi-snarky walls.

But I couldn't shake it off so easily this time. I was exhausted, and I wanted answers. In reply, life gave me a not-so-rabbit research trail named Daisy and a tattooed girl to bring it all from my head to my heart.

```
┌─────────────────────────────────────────────┐
│  ┌──────────────────────────────────────┐    │
│  │                                       │    │
│  │        RESEARCH NOTES                 │    │
│  │                                       │    │
│  │   SUBJECT  Daisy's Big Moment         │    │
│  │   YEAR     2003                       │    │
│  │                                       │    │
│  └──────────────────────────────────────┘    │
└─────────────────────────────────────────────┘
```

Daisy shook her head and impatiently shifted her weight from leg to leg. This was her big day, and she seemed to know it. A nearby television crew fiddled with cords and microphones and adjusted various lights. Daisy was going to sing, and all of Great Britain might hear it.

The British Festival Association of Science was featuring her today, and this would be her shot to show them all. The sound crew finished with the microphones and presented a completely finished recording studio in a chamber, ready to go.[1]

They motioned her forward. Daisy knew she had one chance at this, the limelight, and chances didn't come around very often for girls like Daisy. She was, after all, a duck.

....

When the idea was first presented to Trevor Cox that his academic team should feature a duck for the British Association Festival of Science, he balked at the idea.[2] This was a respectable festival, after all. It was organized by the British Association, and this year Salford University,

....

his university, would host it. Yet here they were, about to feature a quacking duck at the festival.

It had begun with an innocent question from a member of the media: "Is it true that a duck's quack doesn't echo?" And it had snowballed from there.

Trevor Cox thinks back to how the entire adventure started.

> We were contacted by a couple of broadcasters wanting to fact-check the phrase (A duck's quack doesn't echo). We got annoyed when someone broadcast the phrase as true when we had told them it was false. So we decided to do a bit of mythbusting (before that became a popular TV franchise).
>
> They asked me to do something at the press launch in London. I suggested that a frivolous story about ducks wasn't going to interest the press, but the science correspondents loved it.[3]

So Cox's team at the Salford University's Acoustics Research Center pressed ahead with the experiment. Danny McCaul and Emma Shanks fixed the acoustic laboratories.

```
SCIENCE NOTES:

The team wanted two sound bytes: One of Daisy
quacking into an anecho chamber—a room with padded
walls to deaden any sound bouncing around. And
another sound byte of Daisy quacking in an echo
chamber—a room set up specifically to allow an echo.
Then they could compare the two to see if there was
any difference. If there was a difference, it would
prove that Daisy's quack echoed.[4]
```

Everything was structured to scientific certainty. And then it was time. They brought Daisy into each of the two chambers, and she debuted her voice and quacked as only she could.

And because this was Salford, we can only assume she quacked in a slight British accent with the essence of Colin Firth.

The sound bytes were laid out for comparison for the public. And there it was—faint, but distinct. Daisy's voice did indeed echo.

Cox describes the reaction from the press.

> The sounds were funny, and most importantly for the press, the picture of the duck and the microphone was a picture editor's dream. A professional photo shoot was set up for the next day. It became the biggest news story from the whole festival. Discovery and National Geographic both filmed the experiment.[5]

Daisy and her echoing quack had found fame.

....

The myth had been preposterous to Cox's team from the beginning. Why wouldn't a duck's quack echo? But somewhere the rumor had started, and it had spread across the continent.

It was hard to disprove because the best places to test out echoes— canyons, caves, grand empty rooms—didn't often have quacking ducks flying around. And if they did, you didn't think about echoes. You were

....

too busy trying to get the flying, quacking ducks out of the room.

If you listen to the soundtrack from the experiment, you'll hear that Daisy's voice didn't have the loud and powerful reverberation of a tenor opera singer sounding his voice into a grand cavern.

In fact, you have to lean in a bit to hear it on the sound byte. But the difference is there. Daisy had caused an echo.

PERSONAL NOTES

SUBJECT _The Things I Hear_
YEAR _Throughout Time_

I had heard it over and over through the years.

"Oh, I'm just nothing."
"Oh, I'm just nobody."
"I'm not famous like they are, so my opinion's not important."
"Nobody listens to me."
"I'm just little ol' me. I'm not a leader."

And I could see where people had gotten those ideas. The mass media and social media cultures made it seem as if a gajillionty fans and followers were the standard for success. That's what it felt like to me anyway.

Success seemed like two billion people watching you put on eyeliner in a YouTube video, and I didn't have that. I think if I were honest, a part of me wanted that. I wanted to feel as if I mattered in the world. I wanted to echo, to resonate—for my life to make a lasting impact. But maybe I'd lost the grasp of what that really meant.

. . . .

I was on a road trip recently—listening to a podcast marathon and eating fried chicken to stay awake—and ran across this statement by podcaster Clay Shaver:

> An enormous reach or audience does not make you more valuable. It just makes you louder. And being loud doesn't make you someone worth listening to. You don't have to be loud to be heard; you have to be clear.

I swerved in the road and almost took out a construction cone just from the sheer realization of it all. It was true. I knew a lot of people who were famous who weren't doing much to positively impact anyone.

Maybe I needed to reassess my perspective on resonating. What if the loudness of the voice and the huge following weren't the things that were important? What if my beliefs of current inadequacy were beautifully and tragically wrong?

After all, I had seen in my own life how people's actions, even small ones, had affected those around them. What if, like Daisy, we were all causing echoes . . . whether we wanted to or not?

And I don't mean the mindless echoes of people parroting everything we say. I mean the kind of echoes that reaches past our own selves and spreads out like the ripples in a pond and influences the world around us. The kind of echoes that extends past the span of our lifetimes and leaves a legacy of greatness.

What if the real truth was that we were more powerful than we ever imagined—just as the people we were?

....

I wasn't sure whether or not I wanted that to be true. In the back of my mind, I knew it would force a few changes in my life if it were, and *change* was not the most comforting word in my vocabulary.

Were there quiet Daisy echoes happening in our day-to-day lives? And if so, did they make a difference?

I immediately thought of cinnamon rolls; and not just because I was hungry (although I was).

. . . .

```
┌─────────────────────────────────────────────┐
│  ┌───────────────────────────────────────┐   │
│  │                                       │   │
│  │        PERSONAL  NOTES                │   │
│  │                                       │   │
│  │   SUBJECT___Grandma_____        │   │
│  │                                       │   │
│  │   YEAR____Present Day_____        │   │
│  │                                       │   │
│  └───────────────────────────────────────┘   │
└─────────────────────────────────────────────┘
```

My grandma doesn't walk into a room; she sashays.

She has the essence of sunshine and chocolate chip cookies with a side
of bacon, and you just can't help but like her. You can try not to, but it
doesn't work.

When I was in the fourth grade, Grandma worked as the custodian
at my school. Students stayed in at recess just to help her clean the
building; it was the strangest thing. I would follow and watch as I ate
boxes of sugar cubes that I found in the teachers' break room.

Well, this explains a lot, doesn't it?

It must have been something about Grandma, because it sure wasn't
about anyone's love of floors. I mean, those kids were the ones who
put all the marks on the floor to begin with. But they just wanted to be
around her.

She was full of joy, patting the kids' heads and preaching them mini
sermons of encouragement and loving reprimand every chance she got.
Who knows how many of those kids hadn't heard encouragement that
week? Plus, they learned some amazing sweeping and mopping skills,
which I'm sure their future spouses were thankful for.

. . . .

I noticed something watching those kids. They weren't just responding to the words she was saying. It was as if they were catching her joy as well.

Grandma has that effect on people. She's the type of person who could chuck a plate at your head and you would thank her while you were ducking. You just can't help it.

And you're not sure why. But it happens.

She pinches your cheeks and pats you on the back, and it's annoying as heck and you love it. Somewhere inside, you start to smile a bit, and you leave feeling a bit warmer than you did before.

How does it happen? How does your mood change just by being around her?

Her love must play a part in it somehow. Her homemade cinnamon rolls that she's so famous for, for sure. Her amazing spirit. And one more thing. Something subtle and scientific that underlies her interactions. But to explain it, I need to stack a few puzzle pieces up and then fit them together so you can see the picture. And it's a really cool picture.

....

PERSONAL NOTES

SUBJECT __Mirror Date__

YEAR __All Too Recently__

When you walk into a room, you change it.

When you understand what's really going on in the world around you and the impact you have, it will change the way you see yourself. It will change the way you interact with people forever.

This dinner was going well, I could feel it. His dark hipster hair, my cute polka-dot dress, the candles on the restaurant table. I glanced over at him sitting across the table.

His left hand was closed in a fist in front of him, and he was leaning forward a bit to rest on his arm. His right hand rested on his glass, and his fingers slowly tapped the side of it in a one-two, one-two pattern . . . waaaait a minute.

I looked down. That's exactly what I was doing. That's *exactly* how I was sitting.

I moved my hands around quickly and awkwardly shuffled my silverware around. Did he catch what had happened? Would he think I was

....

copying him? Would I end up on *Criminal Minds* as that strange stalker girl who took on the life of the man she ate Caesar salad and spaghetti with? Deep breath. Perhaps I was overreacting.

I looked up to find him staring at me quizzically, eyebrows furrowed in curiosity.

I furrowed my eyebrows back at him in frustration.

Oh dear God, I couldn't stop.

....

It's a pretty common occurrence to repeat someone's gestures without even knowing it. It's called postural echoing—more commonly known as mirroring.[6] We unconsciously adapt our postures to mirror those around us, especially those we admire or want to impress.

We sit like the people we're around. We mimic their hand gestures. And if the person nearby is a close friend or someone we want to be like, chances are even higher that we'll imitate them unknowingly.

And the same thing happens when we see someone yawn. Or even think about someone yawning.

yawn

(Did you just yawn there? Please say you did.)

....

We mimic each other without even realizing it. *When facing someone, we tend to mimic them in mirror form.*

We mimic voices around us as well. I know this phenomenon all too well. I've been known to accidentally pick up ridiculous slang phrases of friends and amusing accents from whomever I've been around. And they weren't amusing to begin with; only after I had unknowingly mimicked them.

We even speed up and slow down our rate of speed depending on how a conversation is going. William Condon found that people could adjust their speech patterns within one-twentieth of a second.[7]

You've probably experienced something similar. If you've ever talked to someone who was telling a sad story, you've noticed that their pace of conversation usually slows down. And without even realizing it, you've most likely slowed down your pace of conversation to match it. Otherwise, you'd seem like Alvin the Chipmunk in comparison, and things would be off. No one likes to have a cartoon chipmunk just barge into their conversation.

We don't just mimic each other at observable rates of speed either—sometimes it's blazing fast. Studies have shown that college students can synchronize their movements within twenty-one milliseconds.[8] This is less time than it takes you to snap your fingers.

People even mimic something called microexpressions. We make expressions and mimic on such a fast micro-level that the human eye can't even catch it. Mimicking can occur at a level so small that it will produce no facial expressions that you can see.[9]

. . . .

But it goes deeper than that.

When people see our behaviors, they do more than unconsciously mimic our actions. *They mimic our emotions as well.*

Notes from Dr. Paul Ekman on Microexpressions:[10]
Macro (expressions): normal expressions usually last between ½-second and 4 seconds. They often repeat, and fit with what is said and the sound of the person's voice.

Micro (expressions): These are very brief, usually lasting between 1/15 and 1/25 of a second. They often display a concealed emotion and are the result of suppression (deliberate concealment) or repression (unconscious concealment).

....

```
┌─────────────────────────────────────────────┐
│ ┌─────────────────────────────────────────┐ │
│ │                                           │ │
│ │         PERSONAL  NOTES                   │ │
│ │                                           │ │
│ │   SUBJECT  Ukrainian  Contagion           │ │
│ │   YEAR     Not Too Long Ago               │ │
│ │                                           │ │
│ └─────────────────────────────────────────┘ │
└─────────────────────────────────────────────┘
```

We change the environment of a place simply by entering it.

I cry at weddings. Every. Single. Time.

I crashed a Ukrainian wedding awhile back. I didn't know either person, and I didn't even speak the language of the ceremony.

Still cried.

The second the bride started walking down the aisle and the groom teared up, I was a goner. (See: box of tissues). Never mind that I had never seen these people before. Never mind that I didn't even know their names.

Still cried.

I got a few looks that afternoon—the guests were wondering why the obvious midwesterner was eating all of the desserts. They probably saw all the tears and thought, *Wow, she must have been close to the couple.*

. . . .

I had no idea why I had cried. I assumed it was because I was a sensitive, caring, and empathetic human being. My friends assured me this was not the case.

It turns out there was something similar at the foundation of my awkward dinner posturing, my crying at weddings, and my grandma's contagious happiness.

Something that gives us all the ability to pass along more than postures and gestures to other people. Something brilliantly frightening that is happening in our brains to give us the ability to pass along emotions as well. It's called emotional contagion.

....

```
┌─────────────────────────────────────────────────────┐
│  ┌───────────────────────────────────────────────┐  │
│  │                                                 │  │
│  │          R E S E A R C H   N O T E S            │  │
│  │                                                 │  │
│  │  SUBJECT  Emotional Contagion                   │  │
│  │  YEAR     Present Day                            │  │
│  │                                                 │  │
│  └───────────────────────────────────────────────┘  │
└─────────────────────────────────────────────────────┘
```

People can catch our emotions like they would the flu (except with less sneezing). It can spread like chicken pox in a crowded kindergarten classroom. A person can change the mood of the people around them. Scientists have a term for this. They call it emotional contagion.

Emotional contagion is the tendency for two individuals to emotionally converge.

Emotional Contagion–

"The tendency to automatically mimic and synchronize expressions, vocalizations, postures, and movements with those of another person's and, consequently, to converge emotionally."[11]

Somewhere in the back of our minds, without even reading the research, we somewhat know that emotional contagion happens. That's where we get these phrases:

You're being a wet blanket
She lit up the room
He's the life of the party
She's a Debbie Downer

The Debbie Downer phrase even became a popular *Saturday Night Live* sketch. The main character, played by Rachel Dratch, added bizarre negative comments to every conversation, to the tune of a sad trombone sound effect in the background. If only we had such sound effects in our real-life conversations—it might make it easier to know whom to avoid.

We've all experienced that one particular person who enters a room and causes everyone to smile. And we've all experienced the flip-side of that: the one person whom you always seem to feel worse after hanging around. Their background music would be a symphony of sad trombones.

It's emotional contagion. The sobering part of it is, so much of it happens unconsciously and unwillingly.

Elaine Hatfield and her team have been at the forefront of emotional contagion research. She was responsible for developing the first theories of how we pass emotions to other people. And being a therapist, she dealt with strong elements of emotional contagion in her own life.

....

Throughout the years, Hatfield noticed how the emotions of her patients affected her. With some patients, she would almost have to fight to keep from being brought down into a sense of gloom or panic.[12]

Growing up a preacher's kid, I had seen something similar. Attending funerals was as natural of a process to me as birthday parties. If bad things happened, my parents were there to help. I saw how they spent hour upon day upon year helping people through their struggles and grief.

Although they brought a sense of peace and hope to situations, it sometimes took an emotional toll on them. They would often have to take time off after helping with a traumatic event to recharge and reset their emotions.

This was a smart strategy for them to adopt, because although they lifted others' spirits, they also picked up the emotions around them. Emotional contagion can go both ways.

How does it work? One theory is that something called mirror neurons fire when we observe others' expressions and our brains produce a similar emotion.

Another one of the theories Hatfield proposed is that when we mimic the expressions of another person, our brain produces a small echo of that emotion as well. And remember, some mimicry is so fast and some micro expressions so indiscernible that you may not even realize why you feel different.

....

She explained it this way: "As people nonconsciously and automatically mimic their companions' fleeting expressions of emotion, they often come to feel pale reflections of their partners' feelings."[13] For example, if a person is angry but trying to hide it, you may not realize consciously that you're responding to their expressions of anger. You may just start feeling tense.

Elaine Hatfield remarked on the nature of emotional contagion and people's odd unawareness of it:

> People seem to be capable of mimicking each others' facial, vocal, and postural expressions with stunning rapidity. As a consequence, they are able to feel themselves into those other emotional lives to a surprising extent. And yet, puzzlingly, they seem oblivious to the importance of mimicry/synchrony in social encounters. They seem unaware of how swiftly and how completely they are able to track the expressive behavior and emotions of others.[14]

Emotional contagion is kind of a big deal. The emotions that we bring into every encounter bleed onto those within our reach. You're affecting every conversation in which you enter.

Something as small as your attitude or emotion can encourage the spirits of those around you. That's a pretty powerful thing.

....

VANDERBILT INTERVIEW NOTES

Interviewed Dr. David Zald today from Vanderbilt University. I sat down in his office and talked with him about all of his research. We tried to figure out which comes first:

Does a person mimic another person's facial expressions and then THOSE EXPRESSIONS cause an echo of the emotion?

Or

Does a person see their friend's emotion and (because of mirror neurons?) have an echo of that emotion AND THEN mimic the facial expression?

The answer is: It's still being debated. No one quite knows for sure the exact mechanism by which all of this works, but they're getting closer to figuring it out.

On a side note: I tried to talk him in to letting me Botox a bunch of college students and perform research studies on them to find out which hypothesis is true. I'm pretty sure if he thought he could get away with it, he might have gone for it. For now, I guess we'll never know.

                        Kinda Wilson

....

PERSONAL NOTES

SUBJECT _Choose Friends_

YEAR _Not Too Long Ago_

I can't talk about emotional contagion without pointing out that those whom we surround ourselves with will have a powerful effect on us.

On one hand, we may want to stubbornly disbelieve it. We want to believe that we can surround ourselves with negative friendships and it not affect us. We tell ourselves that we can stay in an abusive relationship and it not change who we are.

The truth is, if you only hang around negativity, you will be constantly fighting to stay positive. You may be able to stay positive with effort, but it will wear on you. It will tire and drain you.

I heard this question once, and it shook me. I grabbed the nearest sticky note and jotted it down:

> Your significant other will be the biggest support or obstacle you have. Who will you be ten years from now if you become what he or she says about you?

Everything in me wanted to say, "Nooooo! This isn't true! I can be who I wanna be and go where I wanna go!"

. . . .

But at my core, I knew it was true. I knew that getting married and choosing a life partner would mean giving that person incredible influence over me. That was a sobering thought. I like to think I can control my destiny, and the thought of someone else potentially stifling that went against everything in me.

I now look at people and think, *What is this person saying to me and about me? Are they encouraging? Do they give helpful criticism, or are they just critical? This person will help choose who I become. And I want to become someone healthy. And awesome.*

If you choose healthy friendships with positive friends, you will mirror them. They will be a support. Instead of swimming upstream, you will have the current pushing you forward. It's a powerful concept.

"We might speculate that people would often do much better if they recognized how much of their mood was shaped by others' emotions.

Then they could decide whether they wanted to try to soothe the others, wake them up, or avoid them."[15]
—Elaine Hatfield

wow

But a second word of warning: truly healthy, positive people will not allow you to get close if you are an unsupportive, negative force. They realize the concept of emotional contagion.

It is like swimming against a current to obtain a goal or become who you want to be. You may well arrive upstream, but oh how exhausted you will be.

Understanding emotional contagion means that you can intentionally choose to bring positive people close and they will encourage you.

But emotional contagion doesn't just mean that others affect you. It also means that you—yes, you—have a powerful effect on the world around you.

....

PERSONAL NOTES

SUBJECT _Resonating What What?_

YEAR _Not Too Long Ago_

Do we make a difference in the world around us? Like Daisy, do we create an echo even if we don't have the loudest voice?

I looked back over the story of Grandma and the kids and of the mimicry and the emotional contagion.

It was no longer a question of whether or not we echoed or resonated. The pieces fit together to give me this answer pretty strongly: we are all resonating something.

With every interaction we have and every person we talk to, our syllables string together to form subtle arrows of uplift or discouragement. Every word and tone and facial expression is picked up and turned over and reflected or fought. Every smile or frown we share echoes into the atmosphere and bounces off those nearby.

It's not an issue of us making an impact. We all have power. We're all resonating _something_.

I had been asking the wrong question. The question was not just how

....

to resonate; it was how to resonate *freedom*. It was how to take the principles already in play and be a clear voice worth listening to.

This hypothesis started spinning around in my head:

> What if we rounded up everything we knew about being a voice, the power of words, and walking through fear—what if we combined those with the power that we have to resonate?

> Could those concepts stack up and form multiples? If we took what we had learned that had brought us freedom—could we do more than just resonate—could we resonate freedom?

....

```
┌─────────────────────────────────────────────┐
│ ┌───────────────────────────────────────────┐ │
│ │                                           │ │
│ │       R E S E A R C H   N O T E S         │ │
│ │                                           │ │
│ │  SUBJECT  Resonating  Freedom             │ │
│ │  YEAR     Today (and 1950)                │ │
│ │                                           │ │
│ └───────────────────────────────────────────┘ │
└─────────────────────────────────────────────┘
```

When we find freedom ourselves, we resonate freedom as well.

I was onstage singing at an event awhile back and my vocal chords weren't quite up to par, to put it mildly. I should have known better than to pick the song where I had to belt out the verses. In the middle of verse two, I tried to hit the note a little out of my alto range, and I epic-failed it. I knew it. I could feel a collective wince from the non-hearing-aid members of the audience.

Three years ago that whole situation would have sent me into waves of panic and questioning my very purpose in the world. I had been nervous to sing onstage to begin with but had finally worked up the courage to do so.

I remembered the pep talk I had given some of the other singers the week before. "I'd rather have you sing your heart out and hit a wrong note than be scared to sing at all." They had looked at me suspiciously. I could tell they didn't believe me.

"No, really, I mean it. You're going to mess up sometimes. You might as well be yourself and enjoy singing while you're at it." I still wasn't sure if they were buying it.

Now I was eating my words. I knew the other singers there were thinking, *Wow, she really meant it about that singing-your-heart-out-and-messing-up thing.* So I winced with everyone and tried to keep singing.

Now when I mess up at things, I just wince and try to keep singing, so to speak. It comes with the territory. The important part is that I'm stepping out of my comfort zone and enjoying life, even if I don't get everything right.

The cool thing is, when we speak our voice and freely live our lives, it gives others the bravery to do so as well, just by them watching our lives. Just by us walking in freedom, we resonate that freedom onto those around us. And we don't need to be perfect for that to happen.

....

Remember that Asch Independence and Conformity Experiment from earlier? The experiment where some students saw the correct answers but were so doubtful of themselves that they conformed to peer pressure and answered incorrectly?

I failed to mention something.

Solomon Asch kept experimenting with those lines and college students. And in one experiment, he added one thing that dropped the error rate of those conforming by 75 percent. In other words, he made one change that made people braver in their opinions.

He added a partner.

It became known as the Asch Exception.

Solomon Asch set up the exact same experiment: seven to nine people in on the experiment and one subject. Only this time, Asch had one other person say the correct answer. Just one. They called this person the partner.

Error rates dropped sharply—by 75 percent.[16] The subjects would often look at the partner with relief—affection even. Just one person standing up for the right thing gave the subject the strength to be brave and speak his mind.

And the weirdest part of the experiment came later when they added in one random person to go against the majority—but still answer incorrectly. Even though that person answered incorrectly, the fact that they were going against the majority and doing something different freed the subject to answer correctly![17]

It was as if just seeing someone else go against the grain and buck the trend loosed the subject from any societal constraint and fear of looking foolish. They were free to speak for themselves.

When one person stood up against a wrong majority, it made the subject brave enough to stand up too—even if the other person's answer was incorrect.

You or I standing up, finding our voices, and walking our own paths; their effects are more far-reaching than you or I realize. Even when we do not say a word out loud, others see our lives and follow suit. When we Lilac & Magenta it, so to speak, we pass along a little of that gumption to those around us and give them the bravery to resonate freedom as well.

UMP

Even when we don't get everything quite perfect, our lives can still resonate freedom. The power of one. Not the power of a *perfect* one. Just the power of one. (And I just realized that my knowing that gives me more freedom to step out and not be bound by fear! Whoa, epiphany while typing.)

My next thought was this: If we resonated that much freedom just by walking in freedom ourselves, how much of an impact could we have then if we lived with the intention of passing some of it along?

I must have been on the right track. I didn't realize that another scientist had already started down that very road, with wires and electrodes and friend trickery and everything that makes for a great nerd story.

It is more important to imperfectly walk a path that you are called to then to perfectly walk a path that you're not.

```
┌─────────────────────────────────────────────────┐
│  ┌───────────────────────────────────────────┐  │
│  │                                           │  │
│  │         R E S E A R C H   N O T E S       │  │
│  │                                           │  │
│  │   SUBJECT  The Grumpy Professor           │  │
│  │   YEAR  Not Too Long Ago                  │  │
│  │                                           │  │
│  └───────────────────────────────────────────┘  │
└─────────────────────────────────────────────────┘
```

A scientist by the name of Dr. Paul Ekman decided to test the bounds of emotions being passed along when a person was intentionally uplifting.

He was curious to see if someone who was intentionally happy could influence a grumpy person in an everyday situation—a simple conversation. So, being the analyst that he was, he hooked up some acquaintances of his with wires and ran an experiment. Gotta love scientists.

He took one of the most chipper people he knew—a person sometimes referred to as the "happiest person in the world" by the press—a French Buddhist monk living in Nepal named Matthieu Ricard.

Then Dr. Ekman went to his university and found the second-most difficult-to-talk-to professor there. (He initially picked the most difficult, but that person turned out to be pretty impossible to work with. Imagine that.)

Dr. Ekman introduced Ricard to the difficult professor and instructed them to have a conversation. All the while instruments were measuring their blood pressure, heart rate, skin temperatures, and facial expressions. If only my friends would let me try out such experiments.

Dr. Ekman described the progression of the conversation in his book *Emotional Awareness*.[18]

> He conversed with Matthieu, and there was no mutual smiling. Matthieu remained very calm physiologically, but this other fellow showed a fast heart rate and high blood pressure. Over the course of fifteen minutes his blood pressure and heart rate went down, he began to smile, and he said to me afterward, "There is just something about him—I could not fight with him."

Mattieu had changed the environment around him just by being himself and having a pleasant manner in spite of circumstances. He had even influenced the heart rate and blood pressure of the other person!

....

I looked at the story of Mattieu and candidly looked at my life. I wasn't sure I had mastered the art of being someone that people "could not fight with." I'm a little cranky sometimes when I don't get enough snacks to eat during the day. I turn "hangry" and it's every man for himself.

But it was a fascinating realization how much my attitude could leak over onto those around me.

I thought of tense conversations I had been in. When I had let myself

....

be drawn into the frustration of it, the conflict had escalated. When I had taken a deep breath and remained calm like Mattieu, things had diffused more quickly. It was true; I had power to calm situations. Even when I spoke my voice, I could do it in a way that showed honor and didn't invite anger.

And beyond that, the caring smile I gave someone could lift their spirits. If I were intentional, maybe I could even cause smiles on those who had experienced bad days. This sounded like a good challenge to me.

It's crazy to think that you and I have the ability to influence people's moods, but we do. We may not change everything about every situation, but we have the ability to bring a bit of peace into turmoil and a bit of hope into despair.

It takes intention to stay encouraging in the middle of a very non-encouraging environment, but we can do it. We can be aware of our own emotions and be conscious of what we say and how we say it.

And above all, I'm pretty sure we need to actually care about people too, or the whole thing just falls apart as a sham. Our voices and microexpressions betray us, and people can tell when we don't authentically want the best for them.

But if we truly care and love people from our core, our voices are no longer useless noise—they're voices that resonate joy and hope. They're voices that mean something.

....

Looking back, I think that's how it worked for Grandma and my parents anyway.

It was true then; we could start resonating freedom just by discovering freedom ourselves. And we could be intentional and pass some of it along. Not only by our attitudes, but by the intentional words we used as well. And I learned that from an angel in Australia. Sort of.

```
        SOCIAL MEDIA CHALLENGE:

Look back through your last ten posts on
social media.

How many of them were complaining about
life and about how terrible your friends
were? How many were encouraging?

Try this: For the next two weeks, find
something positive and helpful to post once
a day. Once a day, look for someone to
encourage. Send someone a private message
telling them how much you appreciate them.

You'll feel better. You'll attract people
who want to be around positivity, and people
will echo your positive attitude.
```

....

RESEARCH NOTES

SUBJECT _The Angel of the Gap_

YEAR _1964 - 2012_

Don Ritchie got up as he did most days and strolled to his living room window, looking out intently. He squinted a bit to see through the early morning haze. There was no one there. No one to call him out of his cozy house and away from breakfast.

People might have thought Don was just another guy on the street. Maybe Don thought that as well. But Don had a habit of doing something so life-changing that over 160 people thought of him as their personal angel.[19]

What did he do? He talked to people.

Don's house wasn't quite your normal venue. Most houses come with scenic views of trees or lively views of bustling streets.

Not Don's house. It faced the infamous Australian Gap—breathtaking cliffs and unreal beauty. But more than that, the view out his window had been known for one thing since the 1800s: suicide.

It was rare that a week passed without someone trying to jump from the cliffs—successfully or unsuccessfully. And Don did what he could to prevent that.

If he saw someone gazing at the cliffs with that particular look on his or her face, then Don would stroll out to the cliffs and strike up a conversation with them. He would invite them in to have a cup of tea, and they would often take him up on the offer.

• The Gap •

Don had tea with them. He asked questions. He stopped and listened to their stories. And for some, he changed their perspectives. They walked away from the cliffs.

Don said, "I go over there and try to sell them life."

To date, over 160 people have pointed to Don as their figurative fork in the road: their reason for switching paths and changing the trajectory of their lives. And who knew how many people's lives that those people

He said he was inspired by the story of Simpson and his donkey—look up!

had touched as well. It was beyond calculation. Don was eventually nicknamed the "Angel of the Gap" for his kindness near the cliff.

Don was a once-stranger who altered the course of history simply by choosing to talk and listen rather than to look away.

He used what resources he had: talking and tea and a willingness to take a moment to care about the world around him. And care he did. Don considered it an honor to live near the cliffs and to bring hope to people who were hurting. His wife said in an interview, "Aren't we lucky that we've lived here? Because he's saved a few lives."

He lived with intention, with love, and his life resonated.

My life gets so busy with the hustle and bustle of the day that I forget how much of a difference an encouraging word can make. To be honest, I get distracted by deadlines and don't want the bother of losing five minutes that could be put toward checking off another item on my to-do list.

But Don made a difference; not because he was specially trained in suicide prevention (he wasn't), but because he took time to talk to others. He asked himself, Who can I help right where I am? What can I say to encourage someone today?

Author Jonathan Martin added another layer to my ponderings when he said this: "Maybe our calling is to reveal everyone's secret beauty instead of their secret flaws." And I thought that was a wonderful way to look at the world.

....

I pictured myself as a secret undercover agent, observing the people around me and looking for the good things to point out about them that maybe they hadn't even noticed yet. What if I tried to be the mirror to point out the unrecognized good in people? What kind of impact could that have?

The challenge then was not only to choose positive words over negative words but also to choose positive words over apathy.

Thinking about that, I wrote this note to myself:

> Stop. Be present. Look around. Who can you say a positive word to? Ask someone how they are. Tell them they're special. Tell them that they can do difficult things if they need to.

You are placed in your corner of the world for a purpose. No one else can speak into the lives around you the way that you can. No one else can fill the void in that silence as you can.

You don't know whose soul is longing for encouragement in your peer group, in the generation coming along behind you, or in the mentors you look up to. Don't withhold the power in the voice you have been given.

Remember the trace echoes neuroscience study? Think about Hebbian learning and how the words we take to heart echo forward.

That means the things we say to someone could echo in their lives for years. If we choose to speak encouraging truth, then those could be the words that they take to heart.

Our intentional words can resonate life and freedom.

There was one other piece to all of this. Something the podcaster had mentioned about being a clear voice worth listening to. The definition for the word *resonate* also had the word *clear* in it. I had kind of thrown it aside as something unimportant to the whole scheme of things.

But it *was* important. And life was about to make sure I figured that out.

Resonate — to produce or be filled with a deep, clear sound that lasts for a long time.

Manuscript: The Hidden Sort of Beauty

But this one had a look about her, you know? And he thought for once it might be different. There was a beauty in her eyes, and if everyone couldn't see it, he was quite sure he was the last man on earth with true sight. Because there was something good about her in an unassuming kind of way.

He had always thought of things as black or white, but she filled in the gray to a category he couldn't quite name. There are some people I can't put into meaning, he thought. For the first time, I'm at a complete loss.

He had never been one much for waiting for things. This was true. He could tell you the minute he decided upon something, and you could mark the next as the time that he acted upon it.

But maybe some things, some people, couldn't be found in a day, in a fortnight. Maybe it took days and weeks and years to discover the meaning of it all. And in that instant, he decided he could spend half a life trying to find them. Or her.

RESEARCH NOTES

SUBJECT _The Weird Little Ship_

YEAR _1942_

Meredith "Rip" Riddle was only twenty-seven years old when the US Navy put him in charge of his first ship. The year was 1942, and he was anxious to do his part to serve in World War II.

Riddle's ship assignment came in, and he was more than a little surprised. It wasn't a warship. It wasn't a battleship. It wasn't a destroyer. It was a little wooden sailing schooner only 104 feet long, with fifteen crew members who didn't know how to sail. In fact, it had first been used to transport meat overseas.[20]

"He was so surprised when a dockworker pointed out the (ship) for the first time. He was looking for a Navy ship and here was this sailing vessel. He was in shock for quite a while," said Bunny Riddle, Riddle's wife of nearly sixty-three years at the time of her interview.[21]

I suppose Riddle had good reason to be surprised. No one had seen this ship coming. Or little boat, whatever you want to call it.

Authors Marion Hargrove and Herb Carlson reported Riddle's story.

· ·

"It's not just me seeing it, is it?" asked one worried sailor, watching the vessel go past. "I mean, it is really there, isn't it?"

She was a type of vessel that had been somewhat out of fashion ever since the Confederates burned the Norfolk Navy Yard in 1861.

The main boom was festooned with bananas, the cargo hatches were covered with mangos and papayas, and there seemed to be a cow grazing on deck. She was a scrawny specimen, as might be expected from such pasturage, but she was nonetheless unmistakably a cow.

The complement of sixty ships stared goggle-eyed as the vessel passed, and probably the more actively curious among the men assumed that if they had been closer they could figure out what the phenomenon was.

A Navy pilot who had gone out to meet her, and who was now actually aboard, was more bewildered than anybody else. Her name, he knew, was Echo—and it seemed a fitting name, because she was a far cry from anything else he had ever seen in this man's Navy—but nothing else made sense.

Her men wore Navy skivvies and Army shoes. Her officers wore khaki shorts what were neither; they were obviously homemade . . . The Echo's skipper was a newly commissioned, twenty-seven-year-old ensign named . . . Riddle (nickname: Rip) from Shelbyville, Tennessee.[22]

The *Echo* was a US Navy vessel loaned by the New Zealand government under a reverse lend lease. But she was working for the US Army. Like the writer said, nothing about the boat made any sense.

War times had made things difficult and the Navy was looking for anything that could be used in the service. And for the next year and a half, the *Echo* served during the war—often hauling cargo and turning out to be an important piece in the Army's coastal watcher system.

Because the *Echo* was a wooden ship, it made it easy for her to avoid detection and blend in with other ships. She was able to nonchalantly wander into a harbor because of it. After all, no one would have expected she had been deemed a warship; they thought she was only carrying supplies.[23] *One rumor said she was a spy ship! Could it be true?* *Anyone know?*

Although some would have classified her as a scow, the *Echo* refused to refer to herself as such. For her entire time of service, she hailed herself as a man-of-war.

The *Echo* ended up being returned to the New Zealand government after being decommissioned in 1944, but not before racking up some crazy adventures.

Tales of the exploits aboard the *Echo* quickly spread, and the story was picked up and made into a movie script. It ended up being the basis for the 1960 comedy film *The Wackiest Ship in the Army* and a TV series in 1965.

The Echo had at least:
3 or 4 fires
Several collisions.
Strandings on beach,
Mudflats, gravel islands...
Good grief!

The *Echo* had been an unlikely starring role—she didn't look like a typical warship. She didn't even really have the normal qualifications, and the men aboard certainly didn't. But that's what made it such a great story.

No one wants to hear how a gigantic amazing warship briskly set sail and churned through choppy waters with ease. I don't identify with that. I identify with the quirky little schooner that didn't quite fit the normal characteristics of what you'd expect in a warship. And she flat-out rocked it.

I looked at the little ship again. Her differences gave her character and made her interesting. And she didn't have to be cut from a cookie-cutter mold to make an impact.

I don't know that I've ever quite fit in with the "normal" anything. But I'd like to think that I could really make a difference in someone's life and that the stuff I'm made of would be enough.

I was starting to notice that people didn't connect with my attempts at cool anyway. They connected to my differences, my quirks. It was those, "Hey, you? Me too!" moments that formed a bond with people.

Maybe some of the things I had been hiding—the unique characteristics, the peculiarities, the mishaps—were the very things that would help me connect with other people. If so, my formula for success needed switched around.

....

And then last week I heard Speaker Robert Madu say this at a conference:

> Comparison will consistently cloud the clarity of the call
> on your life . . . the screens on our iPads (and social media)
> have become mirrors comparing ourselves to everyone
> else instead of showing us who we really are . . . Stop
> complaining for the pieces you didn't get . . . Everything
> you need is already in you.[24]

And that puzzle piece slid into place. That's how you're a clear voice. You recognize you have been placed in your corner of the world to be who you are. Your voice becomes clear. You're no longer trying to be anyone else, to fill anyone else's shoes. You're just being you. You're free to be you. That brings freedom to you and in turn it brings freedom to others. They no longer see you being a mimic of others. They see you radiating in the confidence of someone who knows their worth.

That's how you're a clear voice. You realize the value in your voice, and you use it.

All you need is who you are and what you have. And more than that, you will impact others *because* you're you—not in spite of it. You're a specially designed piece to fit a purpose right where you are.

Which brings me full circle to sitting at a keyboard, staring at the computer screen, asking that same question again . . .

. . . .

PERSONAL NOTES

SUBJECT _Tattooing Echoes_

YEAR _Present Day_

Does all of this really make a difference? Do *I* make a difference?

I knew what I *should* think after reading all of my research, but that didn't change how I felt. And I *felt* tired and unsure about my place in the world.

I clicked over onto my social media pages and distracted myself away from the question. A tag notification popped up on the screen; someone was talking about me. I didn't recognize the name or the face, but I read the post anyway.

> My best friend and I now having matching tattoos. #hardcore. It means "enough" & here's the story. There's a chapter in one of my favorite books that talks about how through everything, you are enough. Just you. All the ups & downs & dreams & relationships . . . it is all enough. Even when you feel horrible and lonely—you are enough.
>
> The author Kinda Wilson ends the chapter saying, "You are beautiful, talented, and loved, and you are enough!" Ever

. . . .

since I read that, I have thought a lot about how hard I have often worked to be "enough" for someone or something. To be "enough" of a daughter, student, employee, friend, or whatever. But my perspective gets a whole lot brighter when I stop and remember that I am enough as I am. Always. Now there's a forever note to self! It's in Greek as a sort of homage to my Greek Orthodox Church . . .

Wow. The words I had shared. She had taken them to heart so much that she had chosen to quite literally tattoo them on her skin. They had echoed past me and were changing the echo in her.

The expanse of it all fell on me full-weight.

I lost words.
I gained words.
All at the same time.

I felt entire dictionaries well up inside of me and beg to be put down on a page.

I had seen too short in a long eternity. I had thought when the words left my lips that they had dropped onto the ground at an invisible force field line just beyond my reach. That's the problem with us practical problem-solvers sometimes. We think our only solutions are within our reasoning. And we think our only influence is as well.

I messaged the girl and asked if I could meet her for coffee and hear her story. We scheduled a meeting for the next week.

....

She entered the coffee shop with a bounce in her step and grinning from ear to ear. It was hard not to smile just sitting near her. She radiated happiness.

We talked about everything; her story, her friends, her upbringing, and where she thought she was headed in this grand thing called life. She told about the little things from her parents that she noticed coming out in her now that she had reached adulthood. "I must have picked them up," she said, "and now I find myself living them out."

"What about you?" I asked. "Do you think there are things about you that others pick up and live out? Have you seen that happen yet?"

She took a breath and glanced down. "I'll try not to cry," she said.

> I decided recently to just be in love with myself. That I'm not going to sit around hating myself like everyone else does . . . and I decided to tell people the things I liked about them. I had noticed things, but I hadn't always said them. But when you have the courage to notice and say something . . . how much it helps. I don't lose anything by telling them. (And to answer your question) I had a friend tell me, "I learned to love myself because I met you." It's like ripples in a pond (the influence we have).

I waved my hands about in excitement and nodded forcefully in agreement; and told her she had pretty much spoken what I had been writing about and coming to terms with.

. . . .

And all of the pieces finally came together in a beautiful picture. The little things I did—they did matter. It mattered to someone. It mattered to the circle of community I had been placed in. Beyond that? Who knew. I had no way of calculating it.

But I knew that if waves spread out in water at the impact of a stone at the mere scientific presence of it all, then how much more must something like a word fitly spoken spread out and echo into the space around it. How much more must lives and hearts and spirits resonate even beyond the shoreline of sight.

My fingers grew antsy and begged to find my computer keyboard. "Let's do this," they sang. "Give us a chance! Let's take on the world." Every hesitation turned to push and gained momentum.

If everyone knew, I thought. *If they only knew what an impact they had. How their voices and lives are powerful enough to make a difference. To resonate.*

....

```
┌─────────────────────────────────────────────┐
│  ┌───────────────────────────────────────┐  │
│  │                                         │  │
│  │      PERSONAL  NOTES                    │  │
│  │                                         │  │
│  │  SUBJECT  Your Voice Resonates          │  │
│  │  YEAR     Now and ALWAYS                │  │
│  │                                         │  │
│  └───────────────────────────────────────┘  │
└─────────────────────────────────────────────┘
```

You are enough.

You are powerful.

Your life can resonate freedom.

You can stick to your guns and be a voice in the middle of confusion. You can choose to "Meh!" when others don't agree with your calling, and you can keep speaking with the voice you were meant to speak with. And even if you don't get everything right—just you speaking your voice frees others to speak as well.

You can begin to find the truth of who you are, recognize it, and cling to it with the voracity of a dying man on flotsam wood in the middle of an ocean of uncertainty. You can begin recognizing what is healthy and life-giving and placing those influences along your path until everywhere you turn reaffirms your worth again and again.

And when no one else is there, you can proclaim it to the empty spaces and the shadows that you find until even the very air is alive and humming with the electricity of your worth.

You can begin creating the echo of the truth of who you are. Of retraining your mind to see what has been there all along. And rewiring the very fibers of your being to believe that you—average, amazing you—can create and accomplish all that you need to do.

The you that you are without trying, without doing anything extra. That version of you is enough.

You can take a step in the direction you are meant to go, even if you are afraid.

You can learn to leave behind the echoing patterns of mental turmoil and choose to make decisions based on faith instead of fear. You can walk away from the Swirling Vortex of Doom. And when people see the new path of freedom you have created, they will follow.

You can choose your attitude every morning and the thoughts that you hold tight within your mind's grasp. You can choose to encourage or discourage. You can bring anger or calm into a room by the mere raise of your voice or tilt of your lips.

You can give smiles and words that echo and ripple through the emotional waters of those around you. Your tone of voice can influence every conversation you have and every person you interact with.

You have strength in your voice.
You can pass along anxiety, or you can pass along confidence.
You can bring depression, or you can bring hope.
You can bring fear into a situation, or you can bring peace.

. . . .

THE ECHO FACTOR
CHALLENGE

. . . .

CHOOSE SOMEONE TO ENCOURAGE AND DO AS MANY OF THE FOLLOWING AS YOU LIKE:

- [ ] Get a pen/pencil that is red, black, or another color that hasn't been used in the book yet.

- [ ] Write a personal greeting on the title page.

- [ ] On page 85, share a positive truth about the person that they can take to heart.

- [ ] Draw a doodle on page 100.

- [ ] On page. 141, share a thought on fear. Something you or they have overcome, are overcoming, or can overcome, even if scary.

- [ ] On page. 194, write one way that they are resonating in the world (or how they have made a difference in your world).

- [ ] Include a favorite recipe. Because food. (Bonus points if it includes bacon or coffee.)

- [ ] Write a favorite inspirational quote at the bottom of one of the pages. (Bonus points if you also include one in a different language.)

- [ ] Underline any meaningful passages in the book you want them to notice. Include your own notes or momentos as well.

- [ ] If you have a picture with the person, print the picture out, write an inscription on the back, and include it.

- [ ] Add a challenge of your own.

AND PASS THE BOOK ALONG

. . . .

You can change the environment you are in—even just a little bit—whether it wants to change or not.

Take where you are right now—you are enough for your life to resonate freedom.

Live each day with intention.

Take each word in your vocabulary and each interaction in your day and breathe life into those around you.

You have the pieces you need to impact your space in the world. You have enough ability, enough reach, enough heart. Take the pieces you already have and use them.

Speak your voice, be intentional, right where you are, right how you are, right who you are.

And start now.

May you find what Solomon Asch found, what Daisy found, what my friend found, and what I have found.

You are enough.   } Remember
You are powerful.   this
Your life can resonate freedom.

....

NOTES

RESOURCES & CITATIONS

PART 1

Candid Camera

1. *Candid Camera*, "Face the Rear." Directed by Peter Funt. USA. Film. Footage licensed from *Candid Camera* for use in *The Echo Factor*.

Solomon Asch and His Grand Experiment

2. Asch, S. E. (1956). "Studies of Independence and Conformity: I. A Minority of One Against a Unanimous Majority." Psychological Monographs, 70, 7.

3. Ibid., 9.

4. Ibid., 11.

5. Ibid., 6.

Notes on the Solomon Asch Study: Reading through the study and post-interview answers, it's clear to see that nothing is completely clear. This study alone is seventy pages in length. It would be doing a disservice to the human complexity to say that a single variable swayed the answers for the subjects; that simply wasn't the case. Reading the responses, you will see that many times with independence, there was doubt. But there were also independent subjects who did not doubt at all. Some yielding subjects denied ever having yielded. Others were so in shock by the situation that they were trying to process it, which did not bode well for clear communication of their motives. There were patterns in the results, yes. One surprising fact was that people tended to remain independent if they were independent from the outset; they were not swayed over time. In other words, the pressure did not appear to be cumulative. But to derive simplified pragmatic steps from this research would be overstepping the nature of its reach. Instead, I hope the findings will provide a bit of insight into human behavior, and even more than that, cause us to take a moment to look at the motives behind our own behavior and study the way we interact in social settings. I hope by reading the responses, we will learn that we all struggle with similar internal battles. And maybe, just maybe, the introspection and not-alone awareness will inspire and equip us to find our own methods for discovering our voices.

6. All responses were taken directly from the Solomon Asch study:

Asch, S. E. (1956). "Studies of Independence and Conformity: I. A Minority of One Against a Unanimous Majority." Psychological Monographs, 70, 7.

Greek Mythology

7. Story and excerpt from "Ovid: The Metamorphoses, Book III (3), Mythology." Accessed September 9, 2014.

Finding a Voice

8. Friend, Ronald, Yvonne Rafferty, and Dana Bramel. "A Puzzling Misinterpretation of the Asch 'Conformity' Study" (1988). Originally published in *European Journal of Social Psychology Eur. J. Soc. Psychol.*: 29–44. [Box M2871, Folder 1, Solomon Asch papers], The Drs. Nicholas and Dorothy Cummings Center for the History of Psychology, The University of Akron.

9. Asch, S. E. "Freedom, Independence and Conformity." [Box M2875, Folder 3, Solomon Asch papers], The Drs. Nicholas and Dorothy Cummings Center for the History of Psychology, The University of Akron.

This tendency to shift the Asch study results toward conformity became the subject of a study itself: Friend, Ronald, Yvonne Rafferty, and Dana Bramel. "A Puzzling Misinterpretation of the Asch 'Conformity' Study" (1988), 29–44. [Box M2871, Folder 1, Solomon Asch papers], The Drs. Nicholas and Dorothy Cummings Center for the History of Psychology, The University of Akron.

. . . .

10. "Biographical Chapter—Old," 1.
   [Box M2881, Folder 18, Solomon Asch papers], The Drs. Nicholas and Dorothy Cummings Center for the History of Psychology, The University of Akron.
11. "Biographical Chapter—Old," 1.
   [Box M2881, Folder 18, Solomon Asch papers], The Drs. Nicholas and Dorothy Cummings Center for the History of Psychology, The University of Akron.
12. Some of Asch's early work involved analyzing how people give varying levels of value to a quote depending on who the quote is attributed to. For instance, they found that people assess a statement differently when they think that Jefferson was the source as opposed to Lenin.
   "Biographical Chapter—Old," 21.
   [Box M2881, Folder 18, Solomon Asch papers], The Drs. Nicholas and Dorothy Cummings Center for the History of Psychology, The University of Akron.

Asch also explains about his research: "In the 1940's and 1950's, I was studying the effects of group pressure upon judgments and opinions." When discussing the effects of advertising and the fascism and Nazism movements, he mentioned, "Briefly, the problem was this: the quality of ideas, of the appeals that served to support mass political movements, as well as the sale of commodities to mass customers, was notoriously crude. The Nazi race theories and the mindless appeals of advertisers violated the most elementary canons of logic and evidence, yet these methods worked." (Taken from Asch, S. E. "Freedom, Independence and Conformity."
[Box M2869, Folder 5, Solomon Asch papers], The Drs. Nicholas and Dorothy Cummings Center for the History of Psychology, The University of Akron.

13. "Biographical Chapter—Old, " 12.
   [Box M2881, Folder 18, Solomon Asch papers], The Drs. Nicholas and Dorothy Cummings Center for the History of Psychology, The University of Akron.
14. Asch, S. E. (1956). "Studies of Independence and Conformity: I. A Minority of One Against a Unanimous Majority." Psychological Monographs, 70, 11–12.
15. All responses were taken directly from the Solomon Asch study:
   Asch, S. E. (1956). "Studies of Independence and Conformity: I. A Minority of One Against a Unanimous Majority." Psychological Monographs, 70, 7.
16. Ibid.
17. Asch, S. E. "Freedom, Independence and Conformity."
   [Box M2875, Folder 3, Solomon Asch papers], The Drs. Nicholas and Dorothy Cummings Center for the History of Psychology, The University of Akron.

Translations Page
   18. All translations taken from http://blog.ted.com/2015/01/20/40-idioms-that-cant-be-translated-literally/

Giving a Meh
   19. Acts 13:13–45 (The Message).
   20. Ibid.
   21. Acts 13:46–51 (The Message).
   22. Acts 13:52 (The Message).
   23. Acts 14 (The Message).

Shopping Retail Therapy

24. I was watching television one day and came across the mentioned TD Jakes interview. Although I do not have that interview clip, he used similar analogies in several other interviews and presentations. This clip from his website describes a similar aspect of the giraffe and turtle analogy: https://youtu.be/ZU2NHe74qrU.

PART II
The Girl Who Remembers Everything

1. Price, Jill, and Bart Davis. *The Woman Who Can't Forget: The Extraordinary Story of Living with the Most Remarkable Memory Known to Science: A Memoir* (New York: Free Press, 2008), 28.
2. Ibid., 3.
3. Ibid., 119.
4. Ibid., 89–91.
5. Ibid., 18.
   Gray, Keturah, and Katie Escherich. "Woman Who Can't Forget Amazes Doctors." ABC News. May 9, 2008. Accessed February 7, 2015.
6. Mcgaugh, J. L. "Making Lasting Memories: Remembering the Significant." *Proceedings of the National Academy of Sciences*, 2013, 10402-0407.
7. Ibid.

Trace Echoes

8. Harmelech, T., S. Preminger, E. Wertman, and R. Malach. "The Day-After Effect: Long Term, Hebbian-Like Restructuring of Resting-State FMRI Patterns Induced by a Single Epoch of Cortical Activation." *Journal of Neuroscience*, 2013, 9488-497.
9. Ibid.
10. Devlin, Hannah, Psych Central. "What is Functional Magnetic Resonance Imaging (fMRI)?" Accessed September 22, 2015. http://psychcentral.com/lib/what-is-functional-magnetic-resonance-imaging-fmri/.
11. Harmelech, T., S. Preminger, E. Wertman, and R. Malach. "The Day-After Effect: Long Term, Hebbian-Like Restructuring of Resting-State FMRI Patterns Induced by a Single Epoch of Cortical Activation." Journal of Neuroscience, 2013, 9488-497.

Other articles referenced that deal with the effect of stress or fear on memories:
   Schmidt, M. V., W. C. Abraham, M. Maroun, O. Stork, and G. Richter-Levin. "Stress-induced Metaplasticity: From Synapses to Behavior." *Neuroscience*, 250 (2013), 112–20.
12. Ibid.
13. Heaven, Douglas. "Echoes in the Brain Open a Window on Yesterday." New Scientist, June 27, 2013.

Hebbian Wiring

14. Hebbian learning is a neuroscience theory describing the way that our brain cells behave when learning information. Donald Hebb presented the foundation of the theory (although others had described similar ideas before) in this book:
   Hebb, D. O. *The Organization of Behavior: A Neuropsychological Theory.* (New York: Wiley, 1949).
   Although Hebbian learning is known for associative learning, the "process by which an association between two stimuli or a behavior and a stimulus is learned" (https://en.wikipedia.org/wiki/Learning#Associative_learning), Hebbbian theories also suggest that one cell needs to fire directly before the other for the learning to occur (https://en.wikipedia.org/wiki/Spike-timing-dependent_plasticity). Not at the very exact same

time. Either way, Hebbian learning is used in explanations of everything from classical conditioning to plasticity. Beyond the general information, these resources also give a good explanation of how Hebbian learning works in layman's terms and the practical applications derived from that.
Leaf, Caroline. "Your Choices Change Your Brain." *Switch On Your Brain: The Key to Peak Happiness, Thinking, and Health* (BakerBooks, 2013).

A good overview of the fundamentals of plasticity can be found in
Merzenich, Michael M. "How Does a Brain Remodel Itself? Ten Fundamentals of Brain Plasticity." *Soft-wired: How the New Science of Brain Plasticity Can Change Your Life* (Parnassus Publishing, LLC, 2013), 53–59.

15. Hebb, D. O. "The First Stage of Perception: Growth of the Assembly." *The Organization of Behavior: A Neuropsychological Theory* (New York: Wiley, 1949), 49.

16. Leaf, Caroline. "Your Choices Change Your Brain." *Switch On Your Brain: The Key to Peak Happiness, Thinking, and Health* (BakerBooks, 2013), 63.

17. Although this quote is many times attributed to Henry David Thoreau, there is evidence that it was misattributed and was actually stated by Wilfred Arlan Peterson in his The Art of Living, Day by Day: Three Hundred and Sixty-five Thoughts, Ideas, Ideals, Experiences, Adventures, Inspirations, to Enrich Your Life (New York: Simon and Schuster, 1972) p. 77. I have been unable to track down the quote thus far. Apparently though, you cannot, in fact, trust everything on the internet.

Phantom Pain

18. This story is under the Creative Commons Attribution 4.0 license, which means it can be reproduced and abridged. The piece was shortened in length for this chapter. The full-length story by Srinath Perur can be found at http://mosaicscience.com/story/mirror-man.

19. Having a phantom pain or a phantom limb is now a widely known phenomenon. It was described even in 1866 in "The Case of George Dedlow."
"The Case of George Dedlow." *The Atlantic Monthly* (July 1, 1866), 1–11. Available to view at http://ebooks.library.cornell.edu/cgi/t/text/pageviewer-idx?c=atla;cc=atla;rgn=full%20text;idno=atla0018-1;didno=atla0018-1;view=image;seq=0007;node=atla0018-1%3A2.
The phrase itself was introduced by Silas Weir Mitchell in 1871 in *Lippincott's Magazine of Popular Literature and Science.*

20. Nikolajsen, Lone, and Troels Staehelin Jensen. "Phantom Limb Pain." *British Journal of Anaesthesia*, 87, No. 1 (2001), 107–16.

Some research suggests that phantom pain is experienced by as much as 90 to 98 percent of recent amputees.
Ramachandran, V. S. "The Perception of Phantom Limbs. The D. O. Hebb Lecture." *Brain*, 1998, 1603-630.

21. Ramachandran, V. S., and E. L. Altschuler. "The Use of Visual Feedback, in Particular Mirror Visual Feedback, in Restoring Brain Function." *Brain*, 2009, 1693-710.

22. Ibid.

23. Ibid.

24. Ibid.

25. Mosaic. "The Mirror Man." Published July 8, 2014. http://mosaicscience.com/story/mirror-man.

26. Ibid.

Photo by Patrick Brown. Permission to use granted through Panos Pictures, London.

Which Wolf You Feed

27. I grew up hearing this story told and retold through the years. I've heard versions of it featuring different Native American tribes and with other variations. This webpage in particular tells two different variations on the tale and was referenced when retelling the story: http://www.firstpeople.us/FP-Html-Legends/TwoWolves-Cherokee.html.

Losing Me, Finding Me

28. This quote has been commonly attributed to Anais Nin, but Elizabeth Appell recently claimed ownership. "I wrote the quote, 'And the day came when the risk to remain closed in a bud became more painful than the risk it took to blossom.' I wrote it in 1979. I was Director of Public Relations for John F. Kennedy University in Orinda." An overview of the debate is described on the webpage http://anaisninblog.skybluepress.com/2013/03/who-wrote-risk-is-the-mystery-solved/.

PART III
Churning Butter on Planes

1. Wise, Jeff. *Extreme Fear: The Science of Your Mind in Danger* (New York: Palgrave Macmillan, 2009), 18–21. What actually happens in the SNS is so far beyond what is discussed here. As Wise points out, "Pain-deadening chemicals flood the brain. Digestion no longer being a priority, the mouth goes dry, and the peristaltic movement of the gut stops." The hypothalamus triggers the adrenal gland to release the stress hormone cortisol as well.
2. Ibid.

William Beebe & the Death Spiral

3,4. Beebe, William. *Edge of the Jungle*. (New York: H. Holt, 1921).
  The story told throughout this chapter was referenced from *Edge of the Jungle* by William Beebe. This work is in the public domain, and the full text can be found at http://www.gutenberg.org/files/25888/25888-h/25888-h.htm#V.
  Although this story was taken from the book *Edge of the Jungle*, I credit the comparison of ant death spirals and fears to an article by Jeff Wise: Wise, Jeff. "Breaking Anxiety's Bizarre Death Loop." Psychology Today, May 21, 2012.
  He was kind enough to permit the use of the comparison in this book and provide other insights about fear and anxiety in his correspondence.
5. Wise, Jeff. "Breaking Anxiety's Bizarre Death Loop." Psychology Today. May 21, 2012.
  Other articles referenced on ant behavior:
  Delsuc, F. (2003). "Army Ants Trapped by Their Evolutionary History." PLoS Biol 1 (2): e37. doi:10.1371/journal.pbio.0000037.
  Thornhill, Ted. "How to Make Ants Commit Suicide by Going into a 'Spiral of Death' (Which Doesn't Always Go Anti-clock-wise)." Mail Online. March 24, 2012.
6. Beebe, William. *Edge of the Jungle* (New York: H. Holt, 1921).

The SVOD

7. Wise, Jeff. "Breaking Anxiety's Bizarre Death Loop." Psychology Today, May 21, 2012.
8. Schneirla, T. C. "A Unique Case of Circular Milling in Ants, Considered in Relation to Trail Following and the General Problem of Orientation." *American Museum Novitates*, No. 1253 (1944).
9. *Wikipedia: The Free Encyclopedia*. San Francisco: Wikimedia Foundation. "Feedback" entry. Accessed September 22, 2015. https://en.wikipedia.org/wiki/Feedback.

Little Albert

10. The research story of Little Albert has been compiled from several sources, including the following:
http://psychology.about.com/od/classicpsychologystudies/a/little-albert-experiment.htm
Deangelis, T. "'Little Albert' Regains His Identity." *Monitor on Psychology* 41, No. 1 (2010): 10. http://www.apa.org/monitor/2010/01/little-albert.aspx.
The entire account of Watson's experiment is detailed in his work:
Watson, J. B. & Rayner, R. (1920). "Conditioned Emotional Reactions." *Journal of Experimental Psychology*, 3 (1), 1–14.
Accessed online at http://psychclassics.yorku.ca/Watson/emotion.htm.

11. Appalachian State University psychologist Hall P. Beck, PhD, and his team of researchers think that they have tracked down the identity of Little Albert. They say the characteristics match "Douglas Merritte, the son of a wetnurse named Arvilla Merritte who lived and worked at a campus hospital at the time of the experiment—receiving $1 for her baby's participation." If this were true, then unfortunately, "Douglas died at age 6 of acquired hydrocephalus." No one ever knew if he overcame the fears that he learned in the Little Albert experiment.
Their discovery was reported in the October *American Psychologist* (Vol. 64, No. 7) and retold in the following article:
Deangelis, T. "'Little Albert' Regains His Identity." *Monitor on Psychology* 41, No. 1 (2010): 10. http://www.apa.org/monitor/2010/01/little-albert.aspx.

12. Ibid.

13. Quirk, Gregory J. et al. "Erasing Fear Memories with Extinction Training." *The Journal of Neuroscience* 30.45 (2010): 14993–14997. PMC. Web. September 14, 2015.

14. Fear extinction does not mean that the memory of the fear no longer exists but that new learning occurs to create a different response, as the following describes. (CS = Conditioned Stimulus; US = Unconditioned Stimulus.)

"Progress has also been made in understanding the extinction of conditioned fear when the CS is repeatedly presented in the absence of the US. Contrary to common wisdom, extinction is not equivalent to forgetting but instead represents new learning—learning that the CS no longer reliably predicts the US."
Sotres-Bayon, Francisco (2015). "Learning Not To Fear: Amygdala, Prefrontal Cortex And Synaptic Plasticity Involvement In Fear Extinction." Center for Neural Science, New York University.
Also this quote found in the same journal:
"For some time it has been accepted that extinction does not involve forgetting or memory erasure but instead involves new learning that inhibits or overrides past learning." Sourced from Bouton ME (2004) Context and behavioral processes in extinction. Learn Mem11:485-494.

Me and My Vivid Imagination

15. Research has been conducted in several areas related to this, from emotions to even imagining the sensation of being cold, as described in:
Hatfield, Elaine, and John T. Cacioppo. "Current Implications and Suggestions for Future Research." *Emotional Contagion: Studies in Emotion and Social Interaction* (Cambridge, England: Cambridge University Press, 1994), 196–197.

Reframing: It's a Thinking Game

16. From email correspondence with author Jeff Wise who was very generous with his time and wisdom.

Reframing: The Red Pants

17. Although authors Chip and Dan Heath used this framework for general decision-making, I decided to apply it to combat fear in my decision-making process through reframing.
    Heath, Chip, and Dan Heath. *Decisive* (New York: Crown Business, 2013).

Dr. Schwartz

18. Schwartz, Jeffrey, and Beverly Beyette. "Introduction." *Brain Lock: Free Yourself from Obsessive-compulsive Behavior : A Four-step Self-treatment Method to Change Your Brain Chemistry* (New York, NY: ReganBooks, 1996), 32.
19. Ibid., 48–49.
20. Ibid., 35.
21. Ibid., 11.

Me vs. the Mountain

22. Studies discussed in the following book:
    Hatfield, Elaine, and John T. Cacioppo. "Mechanisms: II. Emotional Experience and Feedback." *Emotional Contagion: Studies in Emotion and Social Interaction* (Cambridge, England: Cambridge University Press, 1994), 69–70.
23. Ibid.

The Hook Echo

24. Information for this story has been pulled from articles by Jim Angel located here: https://climateillinois. wordpress.com/2013/04/09/60th-anniversary-of-the-first-tornado-detected-by-radar/ and from this article, http://cocorahs.blogspot.com/2013/04/first-tornado-hook-echo-observed-60.html, which mentions that they have included extra story details from Don's wife. All reports are very similar, except some mention Don's assistant while others do not. Jim Angel knew Don personally and responded to my fact-checking inquiry about the sources used in his article: "Some of the information was documented and some of it is from personal knowledge."
    Huff, F.A., H.W. Hiser, and S.G. Bigler, "Study of an Illinois Tornado Using Radar, Synoptic Weather, and Field Survey Data" (1954). Report of Investigation No. 22, Illinois State Water Survey. (partially included) relates more technical facts regarding the situation than personal ones.

PART IV
Daisy's Big Moment

1. The University of Salford describes their experiment, along with audio clips to listen to, on this page: http://www.acoustics.salford.ac.uk/acoustics_info/duck/.
   The BBC reported on the story here: http://news.bbc.co.uk/2/hi/science/nature/3086890.stm.
2. Taken from email correspondence with Trevor Cox. Many thanks to his willingness to share story details and provide the photographs to use in this story.
3. Ibid.
4. University of Salford. "A Duck's Quack Doesn't Echo." Salford, Greater Manchester, UK. Accessed September 22, 2015. http://www.acoustics.salford.ac.uk/acoustics_info/duck/.
5. Email correspondence with Trevor Cox.

Mirror Date

6. Hatfield, Elaine, and John T. Cacioppo. "Mechanisms: I. Emotional Mimicry/Synchrony." *Emotional Contagion: Studies in Emotion and Social Interaction* (Cambridge, England: Cambridge University Press, 1994), 33.

7. Ibid., 28.

8. Ibid., 37–38.

9. This concept is discussed in Cacioppo, J. T., L. G. Tassinary, and A. J. Fridlund. "Skeletomotor System." *Principles of Psychophysiology: Physical, Social, and Inferential Elements* (New York: Cambridge University Press, 1990), 325–384. As described in the book Hatfield, Elaine, and John T. Cacioppo. "Mechanisms: I. Emotional mimicry/synchrony." *Emotional Contagion: Studies in Emotion and Social Interaction* (Cambridge, England: Cambridge University Press, 1994), 19.

    Further reading for concept in: Cacioppo, J. T., L. K. Bush, and L. G. Tassinary. "Microexpressive Facial Actions as a Function of Affective Stimuli: Replication and Extension." *Personality and Social Psychology Bulletin*, 1992, 515-26. doi:10.1177/0146167292185001.

10. Dr. Paul Ekman is perhaps the leading psychologist in the research and study of microexpressions. This information, as well as a plethora of other information related to microexpressions, can be found on his website: https://www.paulekman.com/micro-expressions/.

    Other recommended readings that were referenced include:

    Keltner, Dacher, and Paul Ekman. "Facial Expression of Emotion." *Handbook of Emotions*, 2nd ed. (New York: Guilford Publications, 2000), 236–249.

Emotional Contagion

11. Based on Hatfield's previous work and summarized in:

    Hatfield, Elaine, John T. Cacioppo, and Richard L. Rapson. "Introduction and Overview." *Emotional Contagion: Studies in Emotion and Social Interaction* (Cambridge, England: Cambridge University Press, 1994), 5.

12. Ibid., 1–6.

    Further reference for this phenomenon:

    Siebert, Darcy Clay, Carl F. Siebert, and Alicia Taylor-Mclaughlin. "Susceptibility to Emotional Contagion: Its Measurement and Importance to Social Work." *Journal of Social Service Research*, 2007, 47–56.

13. Hatfield, Elaine, John T. Cacioppo, and Richard L. Rapson. "Emotional Contagion." *Current Directions in Psychological Science Current Directions in Psychol Sci*, No. 2 (1993): 96–99.

14. Ibid.

Vanderbilt Interview Notes

Discussion information was taken from an interview with Dr. David H. Zald, professor for the Vanderbilt Department of Psychology. The initial interview was based on Dr. Zald's research paper:

Lishner, David A., Amy B. Cooter, and David H. Zald. "Rapid Emotional Contagion and Expressive Congruence Under Strong Test Conditions." *Journal of Nonverbal Behavior*, 2008, 225–39.

Choose Friends

15. Hatfield, Elaine, John T. Cacioppo, and Richard L. Rapson. "Current Implications and Suggestions." *Emotional Contagion: Studies in Emotion and Social Interaction* (Cambridge, England: Cambridge University Press, 1994), 189.

Resonating Freedom

16. Asch, S. E. "Opinions and Social Pressure." *Scientific American* 193, No. 5 (1955): 31–35.

17. Ibid.

The Grumpy Professor

18. All elements of the story in this chapter taken from:

Lama, Dalai, and Paul Ekman, PhD. "Experiencing Emotion." *Emotional Awareness: Overcoming the Obstacles to Psychological Balance and Compassion*, 1st ed. (New York: Henry Holt and Company, 2008), 51–52.

The Angel of the Gap

19. This chapter was compiled from the stories told on the following websites and video interviews:

http://www.independent.co.uk/news/people/news/australia-mourns-angel-of-the-gap-don-ritchie-the-man-who-talked-160-out-of-suicide-7754339.html

http://www.odditycentral.com/news/the-angel-of-the-gap-australian-man-living-near-a-cliff-saved-160-people-from-suicide-by-striking-up-a-conversation.html

http://www.smh.com.au/nsw/death-of-the-angel-of-the-gap-the-man-who-saved-the-suicidal-from-themselves-20120514-1ymle.html

https://www.outoftheshadows.org.au/Home/My-Story/Don-Ritchie

Video: https://www.youtube.com/watch?v=fMpSuK4RKak

Video: https://www.youtube.com/watch?v=o32dxRU2TPY

Resonate definition from: http://www.macmillandictionary.com/us/dictionary/american/resonate

The Weird Little Ship

20. Some sources differ as to story accounts or details. In these cases, I used the most reputable source, which was the book *History of the Eckford Shipping Co. and Blenheim River Traders 1881–1965*, written by H. S. Eckford himself (the company who bought the scow Echo in 1920).

Story details also compiled from the following sites:

http://www.marlboroughonline.co.nz/index.mvc?ArticleID=51

http://www.ussmullany.org/Riddle.html

21. http://www.ussmullany.org/Riddle.html

22. Hargrove, Marion, and Herb Carlson. "Big Fella Wash-Wash." *Argosy: The Complete Man's Magazine*, July, 1956, 15–62.

23. Only one source that I found mentioned using the USS Echo as an information-gathering ship: http://news.usni.org/2015/01/30/unique-ships-u-s-navy

24. Word Explosion Conference, Tulsa, Oklahoma, 2015.

Image of ship By Nickm57 (Own work) [CC BY-SA 3.0 (http://creativecommons.org/licenses/by-sa/3.0)], via Wikimedia Commons

Echo definitions from: http://dictionary.reference.com/

http://www.merriam-webster.com/dictionary/echo

http://www.oxforddictionaries.com/us/definition/american_english/echo

....

ACKNOWLEDGMENTS

SUBJECT _Awesome People_

YEAR _Present Day_

Thanks to my family and friends for believing in me when this was just a far-off idea. Kristian Kelly, Christina Woodrow, Heidi Cummings, Laura Weis, Gillian Ryan, Stacy James, Josh James, Leanne Alyias, Stacy Hendrickson, Lori Heiselman, Chris Heiselman, Randy Langley, Jen Deshler—I can't imagine having done this without having your support.

Thanks to Mike Loomis for providing amazing strategy insight. Shayla Eaton for setting me grammatically straight and for knowing your stuff. Angie Buchanan for pushing and promoting this dream when I was too tired to do it myself. Lori Heiselman for being an unending source of marketing wisdom and encouragement. And the Dreamer and Builder community for answering my never-ending questions at all hours of the day and night and for creating the meme that never seems to die. I can't believe how lucky I am to have you all.

To my first-round readers: You saw the first draft and still stuck around. Thank you for your insight, encouragement, and dedication to helping this go forward. Clay Shaver, Kristian Kelly, John Kelly, Reba Wilson, Chris Heiselman, Mike Loomis, Sarah Southerland, Anna Codutti—you are all amazing, and I thank you.

To Jessica Allée and Sarah Sung: your design work took this from just an idea to a picture on a page. You saw the story in my head and helped bring it to life. Jess, I can't count the number of times you've pulled me from the edge and helped me tackle this project. Much love.

Thanks to Jeff Wise for being so generous with his story and time and the Solomon Asch Foundation for being so unbelievably helpful to an excited researcher. And to Tal Harmelech for conducting the research that fueled this idea in the first place.

....

ABOUT THE AUTHOR

KINDA WILSON

....

KINDA [KEN-DA]

...

1. (noun)
A person who is a connector of ideas.

...

2. (noun)
A person who is an entrepreneur,
writer, instructor, friend, and drinker of coffee.

...

Kinda Wilson is an author, teacher, keynote and TEDx speaker, entrepreneur, and hopeless wanderer. She teaches business classes at Oklahoma State University and loves working with startup companies.

Her latest venture, travelchicks.tv, helps ladies travel across Europe on a budget. When she's not causing epic embarrassing situations overseas, you can find Kinda online, bargain shopping, or at the nearest coffee shop.

To get updates and to hear about more (maybe top secret?) Echo Factor adventures you can be a part of, go to: www.kindawilson.com/signup

Website: www.kindawilson.com
Book info: www.theechofactor.com
Facebook: www.facebook.com/kindawilsonauthor
Twitter: kindawilson